THE MANHATTANVILLE PROJECT

The Manhattanville Project

Teaching Planning Law Amid University-Driven Racialized Dispossession

Stefan Chavez-Norgaard

np:

np:
np-press.org

ISBN 978-1-962365-02-4

Library of Congress Cataloging in Publication Data is available.

Cover image: Columbia University Manhattanville project buildings.
Photo by the author.

For my daughter, Cleo

CONTENTS

PREFACE

I write this Preface in July 2025, as some of America's most hallowed higher-education institutions are under threat. The Trump Administration has recently embarked on challenges to universities' very tax-exempt status and their ability to offer independent, critical curricula and pedagogy. The administration has likewise proposed cuts to Pell grants and federal research funding, and the privatization of federally backed financial aid support. In March 2025, Columbia University was threatened with the loss of $400 million in federal funding due to students' protests against the war in Gaza and the university's response to those protests. Columbia eventually capitulated to the Trump Administration's demands with hopes to restore that funding. Terms of the negotiated agreement included measures allowing campus security officers to arrest people, a mask prohibition aimed at protestors, requirements to expand "intellectual diversity" among faculty, and a top-down "review" of the university's Middle Eastern, South Asian, and African Studies (MESAAS) department. Other universities, like Harvard, remain in active negotiation with the federal administration over sums of money and oversight processes—as well as their ability to confer degrees to international students—all of which might seem existential to the ability of university institutions to function independently.

A skeptical reader might thus wonder whether the topic of this book—university-driven dispossession through the strategic use of land use and planning law—is worth engaging alongside these other, seemingly more urgent, crises facing higher education. Yet I argue that it is. University-driven dispossession, as I find with the case of Columbia's Manhattanville Project and as I argue in this book, exposes the hollowness and frailty of universities' inclusive, social-justice rhetoric. University expansion is often justified as an educational and public good. However, university-driven dispossession allows us to counterpose inclusive aesthetic window-dressing against longstanding, actually occurring institutional practices. It offers a perspective on the administrative and financial priorities of universities and the ways these entities are enmeshed within real estate, high finance, and local politics. And university-driven dispossession sheds light on the callousness of these institutions toward low-income people of color—neighbors—who find themselves "in the way" of campus expansion. Although universities are nominally beacons of progressive humanism, and in the contemporary moment purport to be pillars of principled, values-based resistance, cases of university-driven dispossession should give us pause.

This book provides an extended case study of one such university-driven dispossession project: Columbia University's Manhattanville Campus Expansion. I explore the project's motivations, various actors' resistance to it, and the university's eventual implementation of the project, all from my own very partial perch: as a PhD student, graduate student instructor (Teaching Assistant), and planning law educator within the university's Urban Planning Program. The program, known internationally for its emphasis on social justice in urban planning and its focus on participatory planning and procedural justice, included a Planning Law course focused in detail on the juridical and socio-legal processes by which land use, zoning, and urban-development changes might occur. Given my critical Planning Law expertise, I found that the very university in which I was sitting, Columbia, was a "worst offender."

Yet university-driven dispossession occurs globally, often with devastating effects for vulnerable communities. In Cape Town, South Africa, for example, the infamous apartheid-era racist forced removals of the District Six neighborhood were nominally justified for the Cape Peninsula University of Technology (CPUT) campus. In New Delhi, India, Jawaharlal Nehru University's campus expansion led to students and activists expressing concerns over increased campus militarization in response to student-activists' protests. And in Beijing, Peking University's proposed research center on Yuanmingyuan (Old Summer Palace, a Qing Dynasty resort with historic value) gained controversy over a lack of participatory planning and historic preservation. In the United States, fraught university-community relations and destructive campus-expansion plans have occurred at the University of Chicago, University of Pennsylvania, and Yale University, among others. And even at Columbia itself, the Manhattanville Campus Expansion Project builds on decades of controversial and violent displacement of area residents, including the university's proposed 1960s-era Harlem gymnasium project, "Gym Crow," which was successfully halted by students and activists.

University-driven dispossession, then, in various contexts, reveals the inner workings—and true priorities—of higher-education institutions. Nevertheless, it offers students, faculty, and staff an important opportunity for experiential learning and pedagogical application: students and faculty can apply the social-justice values and political frameworks they study in their programs to the context of their very own institutional home.

Looking historically and drawing on the curricular toolbox of Planning Law, this book encourages "mnemonic resistance": residents, students, community members, journalists, scholars, and others can transparently evaluate university-driven dispossession, remember and archive communities that preceded displacement, and support affected communities in the wake of these projects. Mnemonic resistance also allows affected groups to see any single instance of dispossession within a *longue durée* context of power and contestation, and may even enable organizing and solidarity across various issues or projects, now and in the future.

As the Manhattanville Expansion Project continues to break ground, and as Columbia Business School students enter that new campus to enjoy their gleaming new facilities, I am heartened by the possibility of mnemonic resistance in this case-study context. Despite the power of their university, Columbia students, local community members, and residents from across New York City and beyond carefully documented and vocally opposed the Plan, and ultimately helped negotiate a field-defining Community Benefits Agreement (CBA) as part of their opposition. While the Manhattanville CBA is no panacea, nor does it absolve the university of the project's harmful effects, it can provide a new model for communities as they negotiate with powerful institutional actors, and can allow for marginal "wins" amid the displacement that occurs. I am particularly inspired by the student journalists of the *Columbia Spectator* newspaper, whose articles are cited frequently in the book and whose grounded, shoe-leather journalistic work helps cultivate material to enable mnemonic resistance for future university engagements.

In my planning law courses, bringing my students to the construction site of the Manhattanville Project was a highlight of the course and animated in-class conversations for weeks that followed. This experiential-learning opportunity allowed them to see how principles and processes of planning law can be applied with considerable impact, including by the institution that confers their degrees. This experiential-learning approach and students' accompanying reflections over four years grounded the research process that led to this book.

Lastly, working with np: to publish this book has encouraged me to think about the purpose of institutional critique, in this context and in other contexts. Institutional critique allows us all to find the inconsistencies, hidden agendas, and unstated motivations of powerful actors, and offers a toolkit to contesting and improving those institutions, and perhaps even changing their underlying values or priorities to better reflect the public good. The Manhattanville Expansion Project shows how Planning Law—a course very much in line with what Audre Lorde would call understanding "the master's tools"—can be used to contest, and perhaps one day reconfigure, "the master's house."

Stefan Chavez-Norgaard
Denver, Colorado, July 9, 2025

INTRODUCTION

The Columbia University Graduate School of Architecture, Planning, and Preservation (GSAPP) Urban Planning Program, like many Urban Planning graduate programs across the United States, is committed to research and teaching informed by a critical, historically aware perspective. As one example, on the issue of Takings (or confiscatory zoning classifications) in GSAPP's master's level "Planning Law" course, instructors might typically note both the *rarity* of 5th Amendment Takings Clause precedents, and the *racist historical track record* (and paltry record of "fair market compensation") for state seizures of "real property" that have occurred.[1] Instructors might invoke, in this context, midcentury urban highway projects that bisect Black neighborhoods across America and which were justified using eminent-domain logics. One foundational Takings example, Robert Moses's Cross-Bronx Expressway project, proves particularly generative, in no small part because scholars like Robert Caro and Marshall Berman have powerfully described the bureaucratic violences and consequences of dispossession for residents of the Bronx's East Tremont neighborhood.[2]

Yet teaching Planning Law in such critical historical perspective feels particularly unnerving when sitting in an institution actively implementing a violent Takings project of its own. Indeed, in 2010, Columbia University received a major judicial victory that declared 17 acres of industrial buildings and working-class residents' housing in the heart of West Harlem "blighted," and legitimated university plans as serving a higher "public purpose."[3] Columbia University's Manhattanville Campus Expansion project, which was first launched in 2003, underwent a controversial urban planning process and is now under active implementation; the project has led to the demolition of several blocks in the heart of West Harlem.[4]

On the one hand, Columbia's Manhattanville campus provides instructors with an evocative teaching case and students with a close-by experiential learning opportunity. On the other hand, such course discussions often raise issues not solely confined to eminent domain and Takings, but of American universities' roles in furthering various forms of exclusion and dispossession, particularly of the poor and people of color. How might examples like the Manhattanville project, pedagogically and otherwise, galvanize students and instructors to respond to the complicity of their very own institution, and not merely to injustices of settler-colonial landed-property arrangements more broadly? Alternatively, what is missed by an overly insular focus on campus-connected injustices while numerous seizures of "real property" continue across American cities, often completed with fewer ancillary community benefits? This book draws on reflections from in-class discussion sections with Planning Law students over my four years of service as a graduate student Teaching Assistant (TA), driven by a desire to uncover a troubling disjuncture between the academy's critical theoretical discourse and actually occurring institutional practices.

This book critically engages with the university's Manhattanville campus expansion and the dispossession of longtime West Harlem residents brought about by this project. I see tremendous relevance to universities around the country in the Columbia Manhattanville story, including considerations of serial political-economic exclusion, racial bias, and universities' institutional complicity. I also see in resistance to Manhattanville—by Columbia students and community members alike—important roots of contestation worth understanding and exploring.

Planning Law

"Planning Law" as a subject is a curricular focus at many master's-level Urban Planning programs in the United States and internationally. Master's level urban planning programs—distinct from professional planning certifications and licensures[5]—are governed by the Association of Collegiate Schools of Planning (ACSP) and its Planning Accreditation Board (PAB). PAB accreditation standards are developed with input from an array of urban planning stakeholders and field practitioners, and PAB standards include specific courses, studio and field experience, core competencies, and learning objectives further differentiated for programs at the undergraduate and master's degree levels.

Under PAB standards for "Required knowledge, skills, and values of the profession," planning law—defined as insights around "legal and institutional contexts within which planning occurs"—has long been a staple.[6] Accordingly, many undergraduate and master's courses either offer mandatory "Planning Law" courses to students, or integrate material related to Planning Law into introductory or general courses or other required courses, like Planning History and Theory. Indeed, in April 2019, the master's-level accreditation for the Harvard University Graduate School of Design (GSD) was only approved by the PAB after specific issues—notably the inclusion of a Planning Law course—were addressed and resolved.[7] And as Saghir and Sand argue, the PAB's emphasis on Planning Law has paid off: they surveyed professional planners about their planning education using an array of metrics and found, among other insights, that "The Knowledge competency that ranked highest in both importance and time spent [by respondents] was knowledge of Planning Law."[8]

In the 2025 political moment marked by a national politicization of education and curricula, the PAB plays multiple complex roles. While it can protect planning programs and departments in universities in colleges in states like Florida and Texas, in order to continue with a curriculum that includes planning courses on community-based research and diversity, equity, and inclusion (DEI) in planning; some academic institutions have increasingly argued that PAB standards, and accreditation, provide more of a hurdle or obstacle for planning programs than anything generative. This ongoing debate is shaped by the time-intensive nature of accreditation, the perceived "one-size fits all" nature of accreditation standards, and the waning relevance of certain courses or pedagogical approaches to the field.[9] As of 2025, however, PAB standards remain. And Planning Law remains a staple of central importance to the accreditation competencies for the field.

Indeed, according to data from Saghir and Sand,[10] Planning Law is ranked as the "most important" planning core competency by planning educators, with a mean importance score of 4.87 / 5. Planning Law exceeds all other competencies including study of "The Purpose and Meaning of Planning," "Planning Theory," and "Global Dimensions of Planning," among others. Planning Law is also the core competency on which the most time is spent.

Put succinctly, Planning Law is one of the most fundamental required courses—and core competencies—expected of thousands of urban planning students graduating from PAB-certified programs nationally. And the ways in which instructors teach and students learn this material has a considerable impact on both the field of urban planning academically, and on planners' professional practice.

Yet there are many different ways to teach Planning Law. Some faculty or lecturers might focus on content mastery (that is, memorization of the law and what planners and local government officials can and cannot legally do). Others might focus, more historically, on legal origins. Some might use the case method, inspired by business school pedagogy and employing either real-world examples, hypothetical scenarios, or real court cases.[11] And others might include academic commentary or articles from government officials or activists.[12] Many Planning Law courses involve a mix or variety of all these approaches. Some Planning Law courses are taught by full-time, tenured or tenure-track faculty, but the majority seem to be taught by adjunct lecturers and contingent faculty. This has long been the case at Columbia University, where Planning Law faculty are typically lawyers who also work full-time in legal practice related to Planning Law for a government agency or private law firm. These different pedagogical approaches and instructor backgrounds necessarily have a significant effect on student understanding in this subject.

Lastly, the field of Planning Law—and indeed the field of Property Law more broadly—is a fairly decentralized arena of law, for example when compared with Federal criminal law. As such, subnational jurisdictions shape the field of Planning Law considerably. States like California mandate that cities and counties craft *legally binding* "general plans" or "comprehensive plans" whereas states like New York do not mandate such comprehensive plans and instead enforce planning though zoning codes.[13] Even from city to city, local laws and ordinances differ considerably. The pedagogical approach to Planning Law is often also shaped by academic institutions' local contexts.

Teaching Planning Law

As a PAB-accredited urban planning program, the Master of Science in Urban Planning (MSUP) at the Columbia University Graduate School of Architecture, Planning, and Preservation (GSAPP) includes a mandatory Planning Law course requirement for all first-year MUSP students. Planning Law students enter the classroom with a wide range of personal and professional experiences. Some students, having worked in planning practice between their undergraduate and master's degrees, are steeped in contextually specific Planning Law knowledge, for example related to zoning or land-use law in a particular jurisdiction. Other students, for example international students, may be familiar with legal mandates for planners in their home contexts but new to U.S. Planning Law; these students may also be learning about basic civics and legal concepts—like federalism or the separation of powers—for the first time.

I taught Planning Law as a graduate student teaching assistant (TA) at Columbia for four years, in Spring 2021, 2022, 2023, and 2024, while pursuing my PhD in Urban Planning. Given students' wide-ranging prior experiences when entering Planning Law, I sought to employ a range of experiential pedagogical practices in the classroom that challenged students at different levels of experience. For example, when discussing issues of federalism and jurisdiction, I might request that students join one of three small groups: a group committed to understanding the basic principles of federal/state/local authorities in the Planning Law context; a group that will work to find evidence (cases, laws, statutes) reifying or furthering federalism as a legal concept; and a group that will find evidence to the contrary, undermining or re-working federalism. Students can self-select into various groups and engage material creatively. For example, in such an exercise groups of students might ultimately ponder and make a juridical case for *regionalism* as a multi-local jurisdictional layer, much as Frug has proposed in legal academic work.[14]

In teaching Planning Law content, I seek to pair content that is fairly neutral and basic—about legal fundamentals in land-use and planning and who has authority, with perspectives foregrounding urban planning—with critical academic commentary. The fundamental legal frameworks, precedent cases, and approaches to Planning Law are effectively and synthetically outlined in Rose's 1985 textbook.[15] Other work, for example by Frug, Ford, and Barron and Ellickson, Been, Hills, Roderick, and Serkin, takes the form of more doctrinal law school-style textbooks of cases and authorities.[16] My hope is that critical commentary can supplement and enhance legal material, by engaging legal and historical / institutional origins of local-government and planning law, showing students that legal paradigms are not inevitable, and revealing the presence of hegemonic actors' political and normative choices.

With a critical frame of this sort in mind, the material of Planning Law raises major social and ethical questions about democracy, voice, representation, fairness, and profit, as related to land and urban development. I will illustrate the power of hegemonic or dominant legal paradigms through an example, one that I typically introduce to students in the first course sessions of Planning Law.

An effective way to open a Planning Law course is by discussing property and possession, and possession's constitutive other half: dispossession. A conventional legal approach to discussing this issue might open with the case of *Pierson v. Post, 3 Cai. R. 175 (1805), New York Court of Appeals. Pierson* took place in Southampton, New York, when Mr. Post, hunting with his dogs, began to pursue a wild fox. Mr. Pierson, another local resident of the area, saw the fox as well, killed it, and claimed it as his property. A legal dispute arose between Pierson and Post about the fox: does the fact that Mr. Post was "in active pursuit" of the fox give Mr. Post a property right to the fox, or was it, at that point, still a "wild animal"?

In coming to a decision (and the local trial court and New York Supreme Court disagreed), justices were forced to articulate fundamental principles and definitions about property, and the ways in which property was or was not acquired (possession). The case thus provides an instructive critical entry point for Planning Law as a field, given the centrality of land and ownership to the case.

There are multiple ways to query *Pierson* for students. For example, questions arise such as: Why is it that either of the two fox-hunters have rights, of ownership or of possession, over the fox they seek to hunt? What rights might the *fox* have? Does the fox, a supposedly "wild animal," understand or consent to fixed, rectilinear, property boundaries? What is the origin of possession and how does something "natural" or "wild" become acquired, processually? What does *Pierson* say about property, possession, and land-use planning?

Academic commentary by Carol Rose, Berger, Krueckeberg, and Dorries helps explore these and related questions.[17] Krueckeberg questions property in its entirety by asking questions of "to whom do things belong?" and centers questions of land ownership and the Commons. Berger argues that *Pierson* is *not* about the fox: it is about an ideology (or myth) of American property that we start in a world where no one owns anything (a "state of nature") and the legal system's task is converting that state of nature into absolute, fixed, individual ownership. Dorries adds perspectives of BIPOC Americans who were historically either assumed to be property, collectively murdered in order to enable possession of property, or at best prohibited from themselves possessing property. In each case, the scholars show an implicit *absurdity* to the case context of Pierson, and raise questions about the current moment relevant for students (for example, why do renters have no legal rights when it comes to property-ownership decisions for the settlements they occupy and for which they pay?). The fox occupies a literal and metaphorical role as a "wild animal" occupying a liminal, initially transgressive, and socially marginalized space: the fox is being pursued by two wealthy landowners each making a claim on it, and attempts to avoid capture before it is killed. The case also raises helpful questions about nature, the commons, and common-pool resources, and introduces the concept of a "fugacious resource" (for example, streams, running water, or oil) that cannot easily be fixed or bound on a map. The fox in *Pierson,* like fugacious resources, frustrates Western conceptions of fixed, bounded, and rectilinear parcels with absolute individual ownership.

Over the years, Planning Law students have engaged *Pierson* with a variety of fantastic and creative insights. We have collectively discussed how things come to be owned, the agency of non-human entities—and indeed, following Povinelli's (2016) scholarship, the agency of non-living entities—and the legal rights of non-property owners in the Planning Law system.[18] In my Planning Law classes, we would often discuss contextually embedded relationships between landowners, developers, government entities, neighbor(s), and those *without* formal rights, like renters, children, animals, or public space *users*. And engagements often conclude with an understanding of some of the epistemic and theoretical origins to Anglo-American property law, grounded in a Lockean conception of property and possession.[19]

Later in the course, and inspired by the way Rose, Berger, Krueckeberg, Dorries, and others use Planning Law to interrogate and critique the origins of private property as possession through their critical analysis of *Pierson*, I similarly interrogate eminent domain (possessory and/or regulatory takings) in the field using similar tools.[20]

In Planning Law course contexts, I define *possessory takings* as legal occurrences that involve the physical occupation of a parcel of property, typically by a governmental entity (or in the public interest); and *regulatory takings* as actions with a focus on legal challenges to local regulations that "go too far," effectively reducing the underlying value of private land due to public local regulations. Another way to put it is as a distinction between "physically taking property" and "regulating the owner's use of property," even if that regulation might lead to changes in that property's economic valuation. In broad strokes, I then discuss prevailing legal frameworks and approaches. The Supreme Court used to argue that a regulatory takings can occur if a local regulation does not "substantially advance a legitimate state interest" (and in such a case, the state would be required to compensate private property owners for the economic effects of that regulation). However, "substantial advancement" is difficult to assess, and accordingly today is more rarely used.[21] The new regulatory takings standard comes from *Lucas v South Carolina*(1992): a regulatory takings occurs when a regulation denies the property owner "all economically viable uses" of his or her land. But many courts also use the reasoning from the case of *Penn Central vs. New York City* (1978) to assess regulatory takings. This reasoning, typically called the "Penn Central multi-factor balancing test," involves an ad hoc and discretionary weighing of factors that include the following:

- Whether the land use regulation furthers a legitimate state interest;
- Whether the regulation has an adverse economic effect on the property with no alternative or offsetting reciprocal benefits; and
- Whether the character of the government action places a disproportionate burden upon a single landowner when it should more properly be borne by the community

The *Penn Central* case is worthy of discussion in its own right, given the case's ties to New York City, and to midcentury planning dictates like urban renewal and redevelopment.[22] The case also includes a fascinating contemporary twist: the use of Transferable Development Rights (TDR, or "air rights") which have changed in recent years due to the Midtown East rezoning decision. *Penn Central* thus offers a helpful occasion to discuss the difference between an ad hoc *balancing test* and a bright line or per se rule in Planning Law and legal scholarship, such as the rule developed in *Lucas v. South Carolina*.

Criticality enters the discussion in key ways. First, there are questions of public vs. private interests in land and property. Although the Penn Central railroad company owned Grand Central station, for example, the station was seen as a beautiful *public* landmark by millions of New Yorkers. Who should have the final authority over the use and regulation (or potential demolition) of this parcel of land? In the case of *Lucas*, issues emerge around public access, climate change, and private land—the state of South Carolina sought to prevent development in waterfront areas that were expected to face future "shifting sands" and sea level rise, and allow beach use by the public. And in the case of *Kelo v. City of New London* (2005), issues of public versus private benefit arise. Possessory takings typically require that the state seizes private property in furtherance of a "legitimate public interest," yet in the case of *Kelo* that interest was economic development to be pursued by private firms. Does private-sector-led economic development constitute a legitimate public interest? In a 5-4 decision, the Supreme Court, under the opinion of Justice John Paul Stevens, said that it did, indeed, constitute a public interest.

Whether through a discussion of "property as possession" in the case of *Pierson vs. Post,* or through a discussion of eminent domain and "possessory and regulatory takings," Planning Law seeks to contextualize planning-related laws and policies in this broader political and institutional context. And, perhaps most critically, the course seeks to "bust" a set of longstanding myths about planning and the planning profession, some of which might challenge planning students:

1. That planning and planners once used these tools for violent racialized dispossession, in the mid-twentieth century, but that the field has since been "reformed";
2. That new processes of participatory democratic planning—like communicative rational planning or deliberate consensus in planning—mean there is more democratic legitimacy to possessory takings; and
3. That in a world of "neoliberal developmentalism" in planning, marked by state retrenchment and reduced public

> capacity, planners actually *need* eminent domain to ensure a strong public sector.[23]

Through cases and contestations over both possessory and regulatory takings, I seek to trouble these justifications and narratives, and the moral/ethical legitimacy of the broader field of Planning Law itself.

Teaching Planning Law at Columbia University

As an institutional actor, Columbia University proves to be an interesting and relevant setting in which to study the themes of Planning Law course material. Like many universities, including its New York City neighbor New York University, Columbia functions simultaneously as a university and as a large real-estate corporation. Indeed, the university benefits from tax breaks as a 501(c)(3) nonprofit even as it is New York City's largest private landowner.[24] With over 320 properties, at a combined land-value of over $4 billion, the university's tax-exempt status means it does not need to pay property taxes. According to Haag and Kolodner, over $182 million annually is not going to New York City public coffers because of the university's tax-exempt status.[25] Yet while many of Columbia University's real-estate activities are indeed associated with higher education and student learning, many others are not. The university is a large residential landlord, charging rent for both students and faculty and also non-affiliate community members. The university is also a commercial landlord, renting to small businesses and large national franchises.

Related to themes of Planning Law coursework, Columbia has also used its power as a large and prestigious university in New York City politics to pursue various legal, administrative, and quasi-judicial actions with governments, at both the municipal and state levels. These include eminent domain (possessory and regulatory takings) actions and actions related to zoning and land-use decision-making.

The Manhattanville Project involves one such eminent domain action that is the subject of this book. "Manhattanville," the name of a portion of West Harlem recently re-branded by university administrators and real estate developers, is bordered by 125th Street to the South, Broadway to the East, the Hudson River to the West, and 133rd Street to the North. It is some five blocks North of Morningside Heights and both North and West of Morningside Park. While project proponents advance that the neighborhood was originally home only to little-used industrial warehouses, it was long home to working-class Black and Puerto Rican New Yorkers and is surrounded by multiple public-housing complexes originally managed by the New York City Housing Authority (NYCHA) and New York State Mitchell-Lama Program. The Manhattanville Campus Expansion is now the site of a new, expanded Columbia Business School, and neighborhood demographics have changed dramatically, anticipating and concurrent with this development.

In the Upper Manhattan neighborhood today known as Manhattanville, for example, the University worked with New York City's Department of City Planning (DCP) to pursue a 17-acre "Academic Mixed-Use Area 'Subdistrict'" rezoning and a 35-acre "Special Manhattanville Mixed-Use Zoning District."[26] The Manhattanville project's Environmental Impact Statement (EIS) notes that for the proposed academic mixed-use development plan alone, development would "result in the direct displacement of existing residential units in seven buildings and in two church properties."[27] Here, logics of eminent domain (and specifically possessory takings) blend with zoning and land-use mandates, referred to in the plan's EIS as "subsequent acquisition of certain property within the Academic Mixed-Use Area by the New York State Urban Development Corporation." For many other properties in the footprint area to be developed by Columbia, three different types of "floor-area transfers"—including transferable development rights (TDR), bulk transfers, and transfers of areas from open spaces that would be developable "as-of right"—would give the university great flexibility in construction.[28] For remaining properties in the area *not* owned by Columbia, the plan assumed private market-rate residential and commercial development (and not, for example, affordable housing or housing for low-income renters displaced from their original units in the neighborhood).[29]

The 17-acre campus includes over 12 square blocks of campus buildings, some of which will exceed 20 stories in height. Given that the project involved both eminent domain and a re-zoning, numerous city agencies and departments were involved, including the Department of City Planning (DCP) and New York City Mayor's Office. State officials were also involved.

This is not the first time Columbia University has invoked the heavy hand of eminent domain for university activities. Indeed, in the 1960s, a scheme decried by students as "gym crow" sought to establish a university recreation facility in Morningside Park, which would have displaced residents of Harlem around Manhattan and Morningside Avenues, and reduced the size of the park available for local residents.[30] A broad coalition of students, Civil Rights leaders, Harlem residents, and activists came together to oppose the project.[31] In a Columbia University Libraries retrospective exhibit on the protests, employing primary source materials from 1968, advocates organized a large campus protest to urge

Google Maps

university president Kirk to re-consider the proposed gymnasium. That protest was met with a campus lockdown and police presence and arrests, described comprehensively in *The Columbia Spectator*.[32] Demonstrations culminated in students occupying Hamilton Hall and tearing down a fence that blocked off the proposed portion of Morningside Park dedicated to the gym.[33] The campus' endowment saw severely decreased donations and the university's overall reputation was greatly damaged after its draconian response to these protestors, both taking more than twenty years to recover.[34]

That Columbia's 1968 crisis was grounded most directly in eminent domain, land-use, and zoning law connects directly to the contemporary Manhattanville project pursued by the university. Yet there are key differences. Namely, the coalition of Black neighborhood residents and Civil Rights leaders, a multiracial coalition of

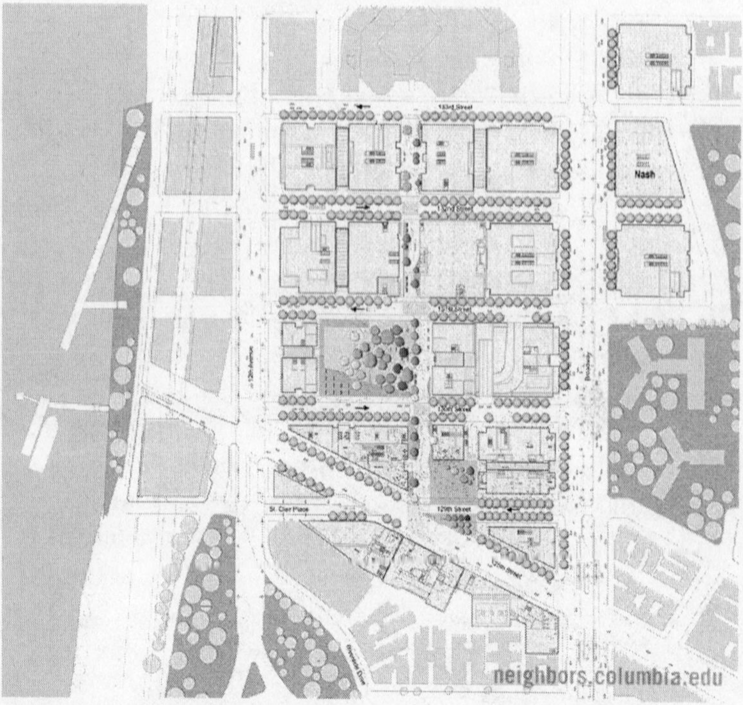

Planned 2030 buildout of the Manhattanville campus. Wikimedia Commons.

students and organizers, and veterans protesting against the Vietnam War *won* and successfully halted the gym project. Writes Eric Mann of this coalition:

> The Columbia University Struggle of 1968, 50 years ago, was in fact a struggle *against* Columbia University—as a ruling class slumlord, a racist gentrifier against the people of Harlem and Morningside Heights, and a genocidal war criminal carrying out weapons research against the People of Vietnam. It was one of the great miracles of the times that students who had been recruited to support The System turned against it and sided with the Black community and the people of Vietnam.

> The struggle against Columbia was carried out by The Movement — a Black United Front in Harlem including Harlem Tenants Association, Morningsiders United and Harlem CORE, the Students' Afro-American Society and Black Students of Hamilton Hall, Students for a Democratic Society at Columbia, and national groups like Student Non-Violent Coordinating Committee, SDS, with support from the national civil rights and anti-war movements.
>
> The Movement demanded that the University stop construction of a gentrifying gymnasium in Morningside Park, opposed by the residents of Harlem and Morningside Heights, who called it Gym Crow, and that it also withdraw all institutional ties to the Institute for Defense Analyses (IDA) — a Department of Defense think-tank that developed weapons to use against national liberation and communist insurgencies including the people of Vietnam. The Columbia University administration, after a two-month struggle, acceded to the core demands of the struggle—an unequivocal victory for The Movement at the time.[35]

In 1968, the university also received $10 million in funding from the Ford Foundation to focus on "community development" activities, which furthered the university's ability to splinter opposition through funded groups like "Students for a Restructured University."[36]

Although the New York City mayor John Lindsay publicly spoke out against gentrification, as well as the war in Vietnam, and famously walked New York City streets to prevent large-scale protests like those seen in cities like Detroit, he did little in terms of policy or mayoral action to halt university actions. Nor did planners, at the city-level Department of City Planning or the state-level Urban Renewal Authority, take any public bureaucratic or political action opposing the project. Yet the loose coalition that Mann calls "The Movement" halted university action in its tracks through advocacy, physical presence, and publicity.

In the 1970s, Columbia University's approach to urban development and gentrification employed more subtle approaches. The university's proposals sought to expand its northern campus beyond the site of the School of International and Public Affairs (SIPA), past the School of Social Work and through to 122nd Street between Morningside Avenue and Broadway. However, countless mid-level residential apartment buildings—many occupied by longtime residents of color—stood in the way.[37] The university, starting in the 1960s, sought to "buy out" these buildings—building-by-building, and block-by-block. Residents organized at venues like Harlem's Riverside Church and through small scale tenants' associations. Junker looks historically at the building level and explores the presence of tenants' self-help movements to advocate for their rights and stay in place.[38] After the 1968 protest, the university publicly committed to only an "underground" gymnasium that did not expand the university's current footprint, and "for keeping all academic growth within present campus boundaries."[39] I.M. Pei designed the multi-level north side of the campus with community relations in mind. Yet quietly the university continued to pursue building-level buyouts of tenants all the way through 122nd St. Even today, the streets north of campus are a patchwork: long-term residents live alongside graduate students in Columbia–owned and managed buildings. Other, privately owned buildings exist next door, primarily housing residents of color.

Columbia's Manhattanville campus expansion plan, viewed in this *longue durée* historical and institutional context, furthered a continuation of coalitional partnerships between students and residents fighting against a large land-use and urban-development actor. Much as with the 1968 "Gym Crow" project, a coalition of activists and movement members protested the Manhattanville plan.[40] As Lau explains, highlighting a coalition rally: "United Front Against Displacement (UFAD), along with campus organizations Student Worker Solidarity and Columbia Housing Equity Project, and students and outside activists, demanded hands off of the majority Black and brown Upper Manhattan neighborhood."

Although advocates did not *halt* the Manhattanville plan, nor prevent university-driven displacement and developer profit, they did extract a number of notable concessions and community benefits for residents over the course of decades of action.[41] University actions, and these concessions, will be described further below, where I contextualize and historicize the university's Manhattanville Project in greater depth. Notable at this stage, however, is a longer historical view of planning as an *arena of contestation,* and the inequalities of power and resources inherent to that contestation. The university's tax-exempt status in fact furthers profit motives linked to its role as residential and commercial landlord.

Yet simultaneously, Columbia *is* an institution of higher learning, and one with faculty and students deeply committed to critical thinking and social justice. Appropriately, students and faculty alike have been on the front lines of opposition to institutional projects. The same is true in the Columbia Graduate School of Architecture, Planning, and Preservation (GSAPP) and its Urban Planning program. Over the course of the Manhattanville project, Columbia urban planners have played multiple, if at times ambiguous roles: as project opponents, as community-relations advocates, as university employees paid to work on plans for the project, as negotiators between university administrators and developers and residents, and as ethnographers and reporters. These multi-faceted relationships create a fertile, as well as a complex, setting in which to teach core concepts of planning law.

A Note on Dispossession, Memory, and Mnemonic Resistance

In Chapter 4, I conclude by pairing my planning, legal, and contextual knowledge of Columbia University's Manhattanville project with personal critical reflections about the nature of dispossession as organized and deployed by American universities. Indeed, drawing on the work of American Studies scholar Davarian Baldwin and others,[42] I consider the extent to which university-induced racial dispossession is a worldwide and continuing phenomenon, one affecting a variety of minoritized communities. What might institutional critique or resistance look like in response to these universities, many of whom are the employers, partners, job providers, and anchors of these very communities, too often on extractive terms?

This book explores the extent to which individual and collective memory and more formal tools like oral histories, archives, museums of memory, and community discussions might enable community-building and set the stage for future organizing and resistance. I consider a concept of *mnemonic resistance*, which looks at the power of memory to introduce new, creative, and emancipatory forms of resistance beyond the more traditional repertoires of community contestation that include protests, demonstrations, or negotiated Community Benefits Agreements (CBAs). After all, while many local residents have been displaced from projects like the one in Manhattanville, many locals still remain. And those affected by Manhattanville—in ways big and small—must be armed with memory to engage and contest the inevitable *next* university incursion.

The field of law and planning law in particular is fundamentally mnemonic as well (think, for example, of Common Law and the importance placed on precedent or *stare decisis*). Much as judges, lawyers, and legal scholars should be armed with historical and case-based legal knowledge to fight juridical battles, memory can serve as the substantive and empirical base for forthcoming community mobilization and organization.

Purpose and Argument

This book uses the case of Columbia University's Manhattanville campus expansion to reveal how racialized dispossession through eminent domain and possessory takings is alive and well in the field of urban planning. Indeed, widespread racialized dispossession is occurring at the very university where the course, with an aspirationally critical orientation, is being taught. Rather than teach about mid-twentieth century eminent domain cases, then, the field of urban planning may do well to look to contemporary universities and their practices. In the case of Manhattanville, planners have used savvy participatory processes to gesture to democratic decision-making, even though plans were envisioned well before such local community engagement processes were initiated. And finally, in the case of Manhattanville, beneficiaries are not just the State of New York and new Columbia University students, but a specific yet wide-ranging network of neighborhood developers, real estate speculators, and property owners (thus enabling and not inhibiting neoliberal developmentalism).

The case thus uncovers a troubling disjuncture between academic departments' critical theoretical discourse, and actually occurring institutional practices. Yet it also offers possibilities: a renewed curricular and pedagogical emphasis in urban planning *criticizing* "window-dressing" participatory planning processes, universities' relationships to institutional power, and built-environmental outcomes of racialized displacement. This can inspire a new generation of professional planners to think twice about such projects, and think creatively about ways to halt or alter them. The field of planning law offers many procedural and substantive avenues—juridically and otherwise—through which planners might intervene.

This introduction has contextualized professional urban planning programs and standards in the United States, foundational critical approaches to teaching planning law, and the historical and institutional context of Columbia University, with an emphasis on land-use and urban-development actions and responses to them. With this overview in mind, Chapter 1 of the book will provide a further overview of my approach to planning law, engaging the syllabus, pedagogical goals, and student activities of planning law in general, and of the course curriculum on takings (regulatory and possessory) specifically. Chapter 2 will provide key historical background and context on Columbia's Manhattanville campus expansion. Unlike the introductory overview which discussed a *longue durée* history of development, displacement, and opposition at the university, this section will focus on the specifics of the Manhattanville project from its conceptualization through to its implementation. Throughout, I will note Columbia GSAPP's ambiguous and multi-faceted roles in the process. In Chapter 3, I will focus on personal and course engagements with this issue in planning law at Columbia GSAPP: having taught a 16–20 person section of the course for four years from 2020–2024, I have engaged this content with students through dynamic discussions, debate, and *in situ* field trips and walks. In Chapter 4, I will discuss and reflect on these experiences and on students' reactions to the Manhattanville project and their conversations. I will also reflect on my own experiences teaching this material at a tremendously contested moment for the university, marked by bungled administrative mismanagement and leadership on many issues and widespread student dissatisfaction. I will note opportunities for *phronesis*, or practical wisdom, in urban planning courses and curricula, through real-life cases like Manhattanville. I will also ask how we, as institutionally affiliated members of Columbia University—graduate students, undergraduate students, faculty, adjunct lecturers—ought to productively inhabit these spaces, as planners, planning law students, and humans. Are there mnemonic practices of remembering what was once in Manhattanville? Are there ways to engage those who were displaced and remain committed to that remembrance? What about neighborhood residents who were not displaced but whose neighbors and neighborhoods have changed around them? Or, alternatively, is it incumbent upon planners and planning law students to take insights and learning to the *next* seemingly inevitable site of university-driven eminent domain and dispossession?

1

THE PEDAGOGICAL BASIS FOR STUDYING PLANNING LAW CRITICALLY

As discussed in the introduction, planning law courses at Columbia Graduate School of Architecture, Planning, and Preservation (GSAPP) are primarily geared toward future practicing planners, rather than toward lawyers or theorists, for example. As such, course objectives include goals relevant to future planners. The course is typically taught with an emphasis on criticality, social justice, and inequalities present in the law, as demonstrated, for example, by the Spring 2021 syllabus of Planning Law, for which I taught a course section as a graduate student teaching assistant:

> Course objectives:
>
> (1) Find and use primary legal sources to understand land use issues and the impact of important legal decisions on planning practice;
>
> (2) Understand the legal foundation of land use regulations impacting contemporary planning;
>
> (3) Determine whether a land use regulation complies with basic constitutional principles;

(4) Understand how the law impacts urban growth, development, and land use patterns, **including racial and economic residential segregation**; and

(5) Learn to **spot critical legal issues in contemporary urban planning practice.**"[1]

Course emphases change with different faculty lecturers and their specific academic disciplinary or professional areas of focus. For example, in Spring 2024, the Professor leading planning law at Columbia GSAPP provided a set of course objectives that were geared toward future work in professional practice:

> This course aims to provide students with a working knowledge of the legal systems and constraints that affect how land may be used and developed and how these systems guide and are guided by participants in the field. With a particular focus on zoning as a tool to implement planning, the course will examine the **issues and tensions that arise** between participants and how **legal and extralegal methods can resolve these land-use conflicts.**[2]

In both contexts, the course emphasizes tools of *phronesis,* or practical wisdom, for students: they might consider using both legal or other planning tools to resolve conflicts that arise related to land-use planning, property, or ownership. And across varied course framings, a common thread of *critical engagement* with the law, especially vis-à-vis inequality, is a strong through-line. Although critical engagement is a strong through-line, different instructors understand criticality differently. I was the only graduate instructor, for example, to foreground Manhattanville in the course and include field trips to the construction sites of Columbia's active project. This emphasis is in keeping with Columbia GSAPP's broader urban planning program, which has branded itself as a critical, and social-justice oriented, academic program.

I understand criticality as follows: to teach in such a way that students are asked to question the values, assumptions, and ideologies (or the "myths") that undergird various features of planning law and planning processes. The planning law curriculum, over the course of my four years of teaching at Columbia, has centrally engaged eminent domain. At times, eminent domain is taught as takings, and separate callouts for "possessory takings" and "regulatory takings" are taught over distinct weeks and corresponding course sessions.

Eminent Domain, Takings, and Planning Law

Course casebooks also choose either to feature material on "eminent domain," broadly defined, or related to "possessory takings" and then "regulatory takings" in turn. For example, the Rose *Legal Foundations of Land-Use Planning* textbook-casebook[3] includes a full chapter (of its seven chapters) on eminent domain, and defines this area of land-use law as follows:

> **Eminent domain**, also known as condemnation, is the power of government to take private property for a public use, without the owner's consent, on the payment of just compensation. Eminent domain is one of the **sovereign powers** that, together with the power of taxation and the police power, is inherent in every "sovereign" government. Both federal and state governments in the United States use the eminent domain power to acquire land for roads, schools, public buildings, urban renewal, parks, or other public uses. State governments can, and usually do, delegate this power to municipal governments. Under limited circumstances, public utilities and other private corporations may be authorized to exercise this power. The power of eminent domain is similar to the **power of taxation** . . . the power of eminent domain is similar to the **police power**.[4]

Rose's definition is compelling because of its simplicity. It also frames a regulating of land or land-use as justified by the state's police power—a rational basis to empower localities to regulate land because state land uses arguably enhance public health, morals, safety, or general welfare—to be distinct from the power of eminent domain *per se.* Other definitions frame *both* a government's physical possession of land, and the regulation of its use that might decrease land values, as a "takings," with different sub-types. Rose clarifies and elaborates: "The power of eminent domain is different from the police power in that when eminent domain is exercised *title* to the property is *taken* from the owner by government and *compensation* is made; when the police power is exercised, title to the property *remains with the owner* but the *use* of the property is *restricted* by governmental regulations and *no compensation* is paid to the owner."[5] *Planning For Wicked Problems*, by Jourdan and Strauss,[6] takes a different approach to this arena of planning law. It eschews the broad language of eminent domain and instead includes discussion of possessory and regulatory takings. Possessory takings, much like the way Rose discusses eminent domain, involves the physical transfer of ownership from a parcel of private property to the state for a nominally public purpose; regulatory takings, by contrast, involves a restriction or regulation on a parcel of privately owned land that diminishes its value. Yet Jourdan and Strauss, in keeping with a strand of land-use law increasingly popular by more conservative justices in federal and state courts, advance that compensation may be required for such regulations: "An owner whose property is significantly devalued as a result of the passage of a local regulation may be compensated. Compensation may be given for both temporary and permanent takings."[7] The presence of distinct ways to teach or bracket different issues is common throughout the material for Planning Law.

Regardless of the specific normative approach to this material, and regardless of the inclusion of regulatory takings as being a subsection of eminent domain or wholly distinct from it, planning law instructors typically focus on the difference between possessory and regulatory takings, including questions of blight and blight designation, the concept for planners of the "highest and best use," issues of the "public interest" in land that a takings must further justify (see *Kelo v. City of New London*), and questions of "just compensation" and how to calculate it. I will discuss each of these issues in turn.

Possessory and Regulatory Takings

Possessory takings are defined as a "takings of property" which is less straightforward when property is not defined geographically but rather as a "bundle of rights" that include use, enjoyment, control, and disposal.[8] There are also questions around the difference between rights to property, "air rights," sub-surface or water and mineral rights, and rights of interest (like joint ownership, easements, development restrictions, and more). A classic example of a possessory takings, however, would be the state assembling parcels of privately owned land to build a roadway or a rail line. Here, the state would seize the privately owned asset and the road or rail line—public infrastructure—would constitute both a "public purpose" and also an arguably higher or better use than the private land alone. The state would be required to compensate landowners for their land.

For a *regulatory takings*, Jourdan and Strauss provide a fictional case-study of the town of Arid, Oklahoma, a small town of two thousand residents, largely dependent on agro-industry (corn) and the service sector, where a recent proposal to explore mineral extraction has created controversy.[9] The town relies on an aquifer for water and for agricultural irrigation, and residents worry that a land-use rezoning to allow for mineral extraction would affect both the quantity (supply) and quality of their water. Here, the residents make the case for a regulatory takings: were the municipality to re-zone land for mineral exploration or extraction, residents could make a compelling case that such a regulation reduced the values of their property, as agricultural land and residential land alike may now have less or poorer-quality water. Accordingly, should these residents be successful, the town of Arid would be on the hook to compensate residents as a consequence of their local-level regulatory decision to rezone land allowing for mineral extraction. However, residents in litigation would need to make the case that their private land values would demonstrably decrease because of the state rezoning, and this would be the amount of money that the state would compensate landowners.

As with the hypothetical above, there are various normative approaches to teaching this material. Concerns over *equity*, *a changing political economy*, *environmentalism*, and *the power of the state versus private landowners* all come into play. Additionally, there are stakeholders not even entitled to a legal voice in this debate: residents of Arid and Oklahomans who are *not land owners*. There are also ethical questions about the long term future of the city. Questions might likewise arise about whether the state, or an extraction company, would be best positioned to provide "just compensation" for the effects of the regulation, which are also framed legally in terms of reductions to residents' property values, rather than in terms of social or environmental understandings of the value of land.

Blight

In order for the state to seize public land, there needs to be a compelling public purpose to do so, and this includes the fact that a given parcel, precinct, or neighborhood is "blighted." In *Berman v. Parker*, a foundational 1950s Supreme Court case justifying eminent domain in the city of Washington, D.C., the Supreme Court upheld a city plan to demolish housing for an area that was home for around five thousand people. The logic underpinning this decision was that these residents' homes were blighted, and not repairable.

In *Berman,* Max Morris owned a D.C. department store that was, by any reasonable assessment, in excellent working order. However, it was designated as "blighted." Suing the state, Morris's lawyer argued that the blight designation logic, which justified blight for the purpose of creating a "better balanced, more attractive community,"[10] was subjective and not valid for public use, and was primarily aesthetic. Yet the court, unanimously, disagreed. Justice Douglass wrote, in the majority opinion: "We do not sit to determine whether a particular housing project is or is not desirable. The concept of the public welfare is broad and inclusive. . . . The values it represents are spiritual as well as physical, aesthetic as well as monetary.[11]

Put differently, the court believed that *local governments* were able to determine metrics of blight based on their own local processes, and that metrics for blight could include subjective measures of "community character" or, indeed, aesthetics. There were, and are, tremendous consequences of the blight designation for low-income communities and communities of color. When communities are designated, in part or in whole, as blighted, tax-incentivized development is often invited and it becomes easier to build highways or large-scale public projects like airports or waste disposal sites, displacing residents. These communities of "locally undesirable land uses," or LULUs, typically low-income, again are far more likely to be sited and built out,. This displacement, then, splinters or destroys communities in ways far beyond the "just compensation" provided by the state, regardless of how one calculates it. Moreover, the presence of LULUs in neighborhoods may further depress land values for generations to come.[12]

Highest and Best Use

Jourdan and Strauss write: "Like zoning, property owners are not entitled to the highest and best use of their lands."[13] Courts typically employ a reasonableness standard, coupled with the traditional possessory and regulatory takings analysis, to determine if a takings is permissible. If, however, one or more parcels fails to approach what planners might calculate as its highest and best use, that may justify planners reasonably imposing regulations or regulatory takings on private properties in the name of the public interest. If, for example, a single-story home is located in an area zoned for high-rise residential development, this factor alone is not likely to justify a takings. That fact may, however, be considered as *one factor among many factors* that might ultimately shape a court's perspective that a takings is warranted. The weighing of these factors, collectively, is called the "multi-factor balancing test," and this approach is described further in the Introduction.

Penn Central Transp. Co. v. New York City is the case where the "multi-factor balancing test" was developed, and is seminal for the field of possessory and regulatory takings in planning law. Here, the Penn Central Transportation Company sought to demolish the historic Grand Central Station, much as they had recently done with the now-defunct Penn Station. As owners of the parcel of land on which both stations sat, Penn Central argued that the "highest and best use" of their land would involve building a higher-density building (a 55-story office tower, to be specific) for which they could charge more rent to tenants. In the case of Grand Central Station, however, New York City's new landmarks law, and the new Landmarks Preservation Commission (LPC), sought to protect Grand Central as an historic landmark. Indeed, the very creation of the LPC and of New York City landmark laws more broadly stemmed from widespread public outrage over the demolition of Penn Station.[14] The court ultimately sided with New York City planners, citing the "multi-factor balancing test," and preventing Grand Central Station's demolition. The court reached this decision through its ad hoc and discretionary weighing of the following factors: whether the land use regulation furthers a legitimate state interest; whether the regulation has an adverse economic effect on the property with no alternative or offsetting reciprocal benefits; and whether the character of the government action places a disproportionate burden on a single landowner when it should more properly be borne by the community.

The concept of "highest and best use," then, is not a legally binding principle nor is it incumbent upon private landowners to achieve. Nonetheless, "highest and best use analysis" is a widespread practice by private developers and real estate practitioners to help these private parties argue to the state that planning rules or regulations are infringing on their maximum possible profit for the land at hand.[15] If private actors are able to successfully demonstrate that this has occurred, they could be entitled to compensation from a regulatory takings. Spool argues that the four tests of "highest and best use" are effectively issues of appraisal, as developers and real estate officials seek to maximize profits subject to four constraints: what is (1) legally permissible, (2) physically possible, (3) financially feasible, and (4) most profitable.[16] Writes Spool: "The first two tests are interchangeable in order and, in many circumstances, the last two are combined."[17] Steps three and four (financially feasible/most profitable) cannot be determined until after analysis of the first two steps.

The first criteria, what is legally permissible on a given parcel of land, relates to issues of zoning and land-use. In the case of Columbia's Manhattanville, many of the parcels in West Harlem were previously zoned for lower-density uses (residential, industrial, and commercial, among others). There was limited potential from the perspective of private developers to further profit from these lands. Yet the Manhattanville project initiated a re-zoning, alongside a large-scale eminent domain acquisition of land and a transfer to Columbia University. These factors may have *increased* the highest possible use for adjacent parcels, as both changes in underlying land values and in zoning and land-use permissions were changed by the project.

It is important to differentiate, however, between *landowners* and *renters, neighborhood residents, and public space users* when it comes to the concept of "highest and best use." Indeed, Madden and Marcuse have argued that critical geographer Neil Smith saw "the rent gap," or "the gap between the current rent and a building's 'highest and best use,'" as "the essence of gentrification."[18] Indeed, writing in the 1870s, Engels used the concept when discussing Haussman's slum-clearance regime in Paris, and connected to the doctrine of what Harvey calls "accumulation by dispossession": put simply, "highest and best use" justifies landowners' dispossession of residents because a more profitable use for land may be possible.[19]

Rarely does the doctrine of "highest and best use" consider, for example, what Newman and Wyly call the "right to stay put," or other non-economic ways of measuring use value and what values might be "best."[20] Rather, "highest and best use" is typically framed as "best" from a monolithic perspective of profit for singular private landowners. Planners and courts have been clear that landowners are not "entitled" to achieve the highest and best use on their parcels from this perspective, but developers and indeed some academics have argued in favor of the concept.[21] When teaching planning law, I typically strive to explain the concept's current normative valence and uses, its non-authoritative legal basis, and alternative possible ways by which planners might consider a parcel or area's use to be its "best," and for whom.

The "Public Interest" in Land that a Takings Must Justify

Foundationally, a takings of private land must be made in the "public interest," a standard highlighted in the urban renewal projects justified by *Berman v. Parker* and countless other cases. But the question of what *constitutes* a "public interest," who decides, and the standards by which courts interpret interests are quite complex. Two foundational cases, *Poletown Council v. Detroit* (1981) and *Kelo v. City of New London,* highlight that what constitutes the "public interest" can be very subjective indeed.

In *Poletown,* the Michigan State Supreme Court ruled that the City of Detroit could condemn private residential property for use as a privately-owned automobile assembly plant (in this case for General Motors [GM]). The court argued that even though GM is a private actor, the site could serve a "public purpose" within the meaning of the Economic Development Corporations Act because jobs, tax benefits, and construction were all associated with the large-scale private project.[22] Notably, the court also ruled that Michigan's Environmental Protection Act does not protect social and cultural environments, but only the physical environment in terms of air quality, water quality, and natural resource management, and as such the project did not have a sufficiently adverse environmental impact as to be halted.[23] The project was allowed to proceed.

A similar set of issues was at stake in the 2005 *Kelo* case, which was not litigated at the state level but rather agued at the U.S. Supreme Court. Here, an individual plaintiff, Susette Kelo, sued the city of New London, Connecticut, for violating her civil rights after the city sought to use eminent domain to acquire her house so that this part of New London could be used for a "comprehensive redevelopment plan." That plan, led by private actors, nonetheless constituted a "public purpose" that included economic development and other related benefits. Major contributors and beneficiaries included the Pfizer company, which pledged to move their corporate headquarters to New London in exchange for massive tax and development benefits.

To aid in Pfizer's relocation, New London pledged to create a redeveloped neighborhood—Fort Trumbull—with upscale hotels, businesses, and housing. At that time, Fort Trumbull was a working-class neighborhood that the city declared "blighted" for the purpose of justifying eminent domain for the new project.

Susette Kelo's pink house made for an evocative image during the *Kelo v. City of New London* case. Although her house certainly does not appear blighted, the neighborhood in which it was located, Fort Trumbull, was cleared for a project supporting Pfizer's corporate campus. Kelo's house was ultimately moved.

In the 5–4 majority opinion, the court sided with the City of

New London. Local governments should have broad deference, the justices argued, to determine what qualifies as a "public use" in their given jurisdiction. In the case of New London, the tax and jobs benefits of the redevelopment adjacent to the Pfizer campus served a "public purpose." Yet opponents argued that the case smacked of "corporate welfare." Huge tax breaks were given to Pfizer for the campus itself and the land in question was in large part not going to be used by, or accessible to, the public.[24] Yet the court argued that "The Fifth Amendment did not require 'literal' public use . . . ," but the "broader and more natural interpretation of public use as 'public purpose.'"[25]

In her dissenting opinion (*Kelo v. City of New London*), Justice O'Connor wrote with concern about *Kelo's* broad framing of the concept of "public purpose".

> Under the banner of economic development, all private property is now vulnerable to being taken and transferred to another private owner, so long as it might be upgraded—*i.e.*, given to an owner who will use it in a way that the legislature deems more beneficial to the public—in the process. To reason, as the Court does, that the incidental public benefits resulting from the subsequent ordinary use of private property render economic development takings "for public use" is to wash out any distinction between private and public use of property.[26]

O'Connor continued:

> Indeed, it could not so claim without adopting the absurd argument that any single family home that might be razed to make way for an apartment building, or any church that might be replaced with a retail store, or any small business that might be more lucrative if it were instead part of a national franchise, is inherently harmful to society and thus within the government's power to condemn.[27]

O'Connor and the dissenting justices worried that the court's deferential interpretation in *Kelo* might allow private property to be cleared for a variety of purposes, some of which were only ostensibly public in nature. Indeed, every private business purports to advance some kind of small-p public purpose: McDonald's advances that as a private franchise it has a public purpose of selling burgers to customers, and Wal-Mart advances that as a private franchise it advances a public purpose of selling affordable goods to consumers. Clearing small private parcels for a purpose only selectively deemed "public" in nature is thus a misuse of eminent domain.

The court majority disagreed, arguing not in favor of Pfizer's corporate campus or even of New London's approach, but merely in the deference to local governments using the tools of eminent domain broadly. Here, a connection to Columbia's Manhattanville Campus Expansion emerges: although the Manhattanville project is advanced by a private actor (Columbia University), New York City argued it advanced a public purpose (research and higher education for the community and a higher and better use of land for the neighborhood). Much as with the Pfizer campus, it is not substantively important whether the public is able to physically access the land in question.

Notes McGeehan, less than five years after the controversial decision, Pfizer backed out of the project completely. The Fort Trumbull area had already been cleared and slated for the firm's new corporate campus. It remains today a largely vacant tract of land. Writes McGeehan: "Pfizer said it would pull 1,400 jobs out of New London within two years and move most of them a few miles away to a campus it owns in Groton, Conn., as a cost-cutting measure. It would leave behind the city's biggest office complex and an adjacent swath of barren land that was cleared of dozens of homes to make room for a hotel, stores and condominiums that were never built."[28]

"Just Compensation" and How to Calculate It

As per the Constitution's fifth amendment, when a possessory taking does occur in full, or when a court rules that a regulatory taking has occurred that reduces a private property's land value in part, the state must provide that landowner *just compensation.* Yet there are various approaches to calculating just compensation, each of which might typically generate a different numerical value. A "battle of the experts"—in which both plaintiffs and defendants engage experts whose analytical processes and conclusions best support their clients' interest—may then occur. A jury and then judge will typically decide on a level of compensation within the bounds of experts' perspectives.

Rose writes that "just compensation has been defined as the full equivalent in money for the value of the property taken.[29] The 'full equivalent in money' has been defined as the market value of the property. Market value, in turn, has been defined as the price that a buyer, willing and able, but not obliged to buy, would pay to a seller, willing and able, but not obliged to sell."[30] Accordingly, the task of calculating just compensation relates to market value, and there are at least four distinct approaches to making that calculation: comparable sales, capitalization of income, reduction of cost less depreciation, and highest and best use (typically reserved for cases when there is vacant or undeveloped land).

The "comparable sales" approach involves gathering evidence related to either selling prices, or real market transactions, for comparable properties in the local market. For example, if a four-story residential building in West Harlem just West of Broadway (now

Manhattanville) were to be acquired through eminent domain, planners could consider recent transactions for similar apartment buildings just east of Broadway that did not experience eminent domain. According to Rose, buildings comparable in construction, condition, location, and time will stand the best chance of serving as a comparable site.[31]

An alternative method, the "capitalization of income," was at play in the case *State of Louisiana, Dept. of Highways v. Crow (1973).* Here, the trial court argued that there were "dissimilarities" with other comparable parcels taken for Louisiana highways and as such the comparable sales approach would not be appropriate.[32] The capitalization of income approach involves using the annual income generated from a building and the rate of return to capital that landowners expect to receive for a building to calculate the "principle," or market value, of that building. The rate of return is also known as the "cap rate" or "capitalization rate" and itself varies with interest rates, rates of return for alternative investments, and other factors. It can be difficult and indeed subjective to calculate. Using this approach, the formula planners might calculate "just compensation" as follows:

income = principle x rate of return

i = p x r

If a court or experts found that a building owner generated \$30,000 annually from a building, and if the expected rate of return to capital for investors in a particular city at a particular time were 10%, the capitalization of income would be as follows:

i = \$30,000 = p x (0.10)

\$30,000 = 0.10*p

p = \$30,000/0.10=\$300,000

In the court case of *Denver Urban Renewal Authority v. Cook* (1974), a dry goods store near Larimer Square in downtown Denver sought to use their gross sales to advocate for a higher rental value statistic in their calculation for just compensation. However, the court in this case ruled that such evidence is *not* admissible, justifying their reasoning by saying that: "We believe that gross sales like profits are more inextricably tied to the management and administration of a business than to the value of the property upon which the business is situated. The same reasons that cause the amount of profits to be an inappropriate measure of the value of the land are applicable to the use of gross sales figures, albeit to a lesser degree."[33] Ultimately, the court used a capitalization of income, and not a gross sales, approach to calculate just compensation, with two "valuation experts" battling over final details.

A third approach to calculating just compensation involves "reproduction cost less depreciation," and is reserved for issues of *specialty*. For example, if there were a fairly unique business or facility—Rose uses the case of a brewery—in a given geography, neither comparable sales nor a capitalization of income would effectively allow for a just compensation calculation to occur because the brewing facility was custom-designed for a very specific function, and as such its income alone would not accurately reflect the costs or benefits of reproducing such a facility elsewhere. Here, valuation appraisers can consider the life expectancy of the current accommodation or facility, and the expected cost of re-building the facility elsewhere, and take the difference. If, for example, if would cost $1 million to rebuild the brewery elsewhere, and if the facility was twenty years old and had a sixty year lifespan, then the reproduction cost less income would be as follows:

$1,000,000-[(20/60)*(1,000,000)]=$1,000,000-$333,333,.33-$666,666.67.

Highest and best use—where experts account for a given parcel's maximum potential value given zoning, land-use, and other regulatory factors—typically is only used for vacant or unbuilt parcels. This is because there is practical and institutional inertia preventing a parcel's highest and best use from being reached whenever a real site has already been constructed. As such, this approach to calculating just compensation is fairly uncommon. In the case of *Masheter v. Oido Holding Co.* (1973), vacant land for Franklin County, Ohio's I-270 highway improvements had a given current value but all expert witnesses expected that value to change pending future changes to the county's land-use scheme. As such, the land would best be held for future development. Here, the recommended just compensation by the jury was too low, given that the highest and best use of the land would increase after an expected forthcoming zoning change.

When experts negotiate over just compensation, individual landowners' battles are often lost from the start. If these landowners were willing to accept alternative arrangements, they typically would have already done so before a court trial involving experts and a jury. For those who Michael Heller calls "the holdouts," there are typically reasons why: a perceived "unfair deal," a battle of principle, or perhaps emotional or community attachment and nostalgia.[34] Regardless of the method by which experts calculate just compensation, and regardless of the numerical assumptions used, rarely does compensation equate to actual current land values, or even what private landowners might have received through bilateral negotiation.

In planning law coursework, I strive to teach all of these methods of calculating just compensation from eminent domain, and to work with students on real-world examples or fictionalized hypotheticals to mimic the process of calculation. Indeed, a hypothetical "battle of experts" has even occurred within the planning law classroom as students make differentiated cases about property values. Throughout these discussions, I try to remind students about power differentials across parties, for example between individual landowners and large corporations or the state. But left entirely out of the conversation are renters, neighborhood residents, and *users* of public space.

2
MANHATTANVILLE CAMPUS EXPANSION IN HISTORICAL CONTEXT

This section examines the specifics of the Manhattanville project from its conceptualization in 2003 through to its ongoing implementation. Throughout, I consider Columbia GSAPP's ambiguous and multi-faceted roles in the process, and specifically the role of GSAPP's social-justice oriented Urban Planning Program, of which I was a part.

The Manhattanville Campus Expansion on Its Face

In the words of Columbia administration through the university-produced publication *Columbia Magazine,* Manhattanville is a "bold vision for a new city campus" and a "21st-Century Campus."[1] Renowned Italian Architect Renzo Piano and his Building Workshop Practice designed a number of Manhattanville buildings and Piano's architectural approach is often highlighted in university promotional materials. Piano was also involved in architecture and urban design for Paris's Centre Pompidou, The Shard in London, the Istanbul Museum of Modern Art, the Auditorium Parco della Musica in Rome, and the California Academy of Sciences, among other sites. In an essay reproduced by *Columbia Magazine*, Piano reflects on the historic weight of the Manhattanville campus, and its symbolic meaning. He writes:

> If you are lucky as an architect, you may get an opportunity at some point in your career to design a building that reflects a shift in society. You need to be in the right place at the right time. When I was very young, more than forty years ago, I had such an opportunity when I was chosen to design the Centre Georges Pompidou, the home of France's national museum of modern art in Paris. . . . I feel that my team's work for Columbia is similarly exciting, since the final product will likely be seen as proposing answers to two profound questions: What should a twenty-first century university campus look like? And how should urban universities, in particular, relate physically to their host cities?

Piano worked on the campus alongside some of the world's top architecture and design firms, including Skidmore, Owings & Merrill, in 2003. SOM has been responsible for many of the twentieth century's most notable building projects, from Chicago's John Hancock Center and Sears / Willis Tower to the recent Moynihan Trail Hall abutting Penn Station in New York City. In answering his rhetorical questions, "What should a twenty-first-century university campus look like? And how should urban universities, in particular, relate physically to their host cities?", Piano sought to contrast the Manhattanville campus with Columbia's existing, nineteenth century Morningside campus. While the Morningside campus is known for its wrought iron gates sequestering campus from the surrounding neighborhood, Piano vowed that in Manhattanville there would be "a radical degree of openness, transparency, and accessibility" and that "no gates or walls will encircle this new campus."[2] Piano also vowed that all building's first floors will be open to the public and act as accessible, community spaces.

Manhattanville is, according to the executive summary of the project, "the largest and most ambitious capital project undertaken by Columbia University since its landmark Morningside Heights campus."[3] And while the university's project description documents highlight adaptive re-use of historic industrial buildings as part of the project, many of the new campus buildings are completely new projects from the ground up. The following buildings form the core of the project:

- The Jerome L. Greene Science Center: This large university-wide research lab contains The Zuckerman Institute for neuroscientific research, a Zuckerman Mind Brain Behavior Institute, a year-round publicly accessible Education Lab (hosting occasional programming for local K-12 students), and public ground-floor amenities including a coffee shop, rock-climbing gym, and local market.
- The Lenfest Center for the Arts: The building contains a large exhibition and performance space, the Wallach Art Gallery, a 150-seat theater and screening room, a skylit open space for events and conversations, and an area known as "The Plaza," a privately owned public space (POPS) for which there is public access.[4]
- The Forum: A building that hosts Columbia World Projects, the cohort of Obama Foundation Scholars, and the Columbia Climate School. The building, at the corner of 125th St. and Broadway, is for many the first glimpse of the Manhattanville campus. The building also has a 430-seat auditorium, large lobby, and café.
- Columbia Business School: A large, multi-building campus, the Columbia Business School campus includes large windows and state-of-the-art classrooms. Notably, Geffen Hall's "Innovation Lab" is host to a "Columbia-Harlem

Small Business Development Center," and a forthcoming café and retail space in Geffen Hall will nominally be open to the public. Kravis Hall hosts business school classrooms and common spaces.

- The Square: This publicly accessible green space is meant to "emphasize accessibility and openness,"[5] with a "social ring" and "woodland walk," and a set of pedestrian passageways for those walking between buildings. Different corner areas, with hard surfaces, are designed for public gathering. The Square both responds to project demands over public and accessible space through the New York City planning process, and to benefits like including public space in the project design.

The images that follow provide both renderings and official photos of the Manhattanville campus buildings. The Columbia University communications team has been well aware of criticism of the campus expansion, and as such has consistently framed the project's public and community benefits in promotional materials. Notes Piano is his university essay: "The goal is to make the campus inviting to neighbors as well as to provide a scenic path to the new West Harlem Piers Park, which Columbia helps to maintain along the Hudson River waterfront."[6] The university has committed ambitious resources to the campus project, and to various community-based collaborations. Motives are mixed for such strategic communications: on the one hand, Columbia surely seeks to be a good neighbor, and build connections with nearby residents, institutions, and community centers. But on the other hand, such public neighborliness was statutorily obligated by way of extensive community negotiations and negotiations with private landowners and residents in West Harlem. Columbia GSAPP, and in particular its urban planning program, played a major role in such negotiations and agreements.

Negotiating with Landowners, and Invoking a Possessory Takings

Columbia University's communication materials highlight dedicated public spaces and an "urban layer." There are legal reasons for this emphasis, the result of extended multi-year negotiations with local community organizations and resident groups. There are also planning-related reasons and associated institutional benefits for the university for agreeing to these elements of the plan, required by New York City's Department of City Planning (DCP). In an exceptional longform article in Columbia's student-run campus newspaper, *The Spectator*, Kilgore-Brown and Milligan (2023) write: "Columbia promised Manhattanville campus space to the community. Accessing it is another story."[7] They highlight the university's 50-page Community Benefits Agreement, signed in 2009, and how to-date only some $400,000 of the required $20 million of CBA set-aside money has been used for Columbia community events and public engagements. Cormier (2009) examines how the CBA was mandated, at the time, by the Bloomberg Administration, and was indeed a condition tied to the university's use of eminent domain to acquire remaining parcels.[8] Kilgore-Brown and Milligan interviewed local residents and artists, who responded with cynicism about the university's offerings. One interviewee, a local artist named Dionis Ortiz, was born and raised in West Harlem and said that while the CBA's agreement promised "some space that can serve some artists," it was not nearly enough for any kind of sustainable community relationships or partnerships. "How many people is [the studio space promised through the CBA] really going to serve?" Ortiz said in the *Spectator* interview.[9] "That, to me, it just feels like a nice way of saying, 'Hey, we did something for you, okay. We gave you a quarter out of the millions

Columbia University Manhattanville project buildings. At top, renderings and design sketches of the Science Center, Lenfest Center for the Arts, and the Forum, all from the Renzo Piano Building Workshop.[1] At right, official building photos from the university of the Science Center, Lenfest Center, and Business School campus.[2]

that we make.'" Ortiz went on to propose alternative community partnerships that he thought would have been more equitable and sustainable, such as teaching opportunities, business management assistance, or support of artists' ongoing or permanent studio practices. Another local resident and visual artist based in West Harlem, Gwendolyn Black, said in an interview with *The Spectator* that she had tried to request space in the Lenfest Center and got a "flat-out" rejection. McKee argues that "Columbia's tax exemptions exceed its annual community investment by millions,"[10] and that while "the seven other Ivy League schools elect to make voluntary payments directly to their local governments in lieu of property taxes . . . Columbia, on the other hand, has long cited its 2009 West Harlem Community Benefits Agreement—a 50-page document outlining monetary commitments to the neighborhood—as its answer to local investment" instead.[11] Put differently, Columbia's CBA agreement is *not* merely altruistic. Given that Columbia's property tax exemptions greatly outpace its CBA obligations, the university is saving money on this deal. And to-date, although most of the campus's private buildings have been completed, many of the POPS and public access spaces are still under construction. As of 2023, McKee argues that only one of six such spaces are actively usable to the public.

The university's CBA requirements are a result of the possessory takings and eminent domain process, as well as negotiations with both individual landowners and community organizations. In the case of the Manhattanville campus expansion, Daar notes an irony: long *before* working with New York City and New York State to declare areas of West Harlem "blighted," Columbia sought to "buy out" property owners on a building-by-building basis.[12] Many agreed to do so, under implicit or explicit threat of the eminent domain actions that were articulated as inevitably to come. For those that did not, it was clear that the value Columbia offered was not sufficient to these businesses. "Fair market value" can rarely encompass social or emotional value, let alone the traumatic costs of dispossession and relocation. For these and other reasons, in the wake of *Kelo* many states have since enacted laws encouraging 150%+ of "fair market value" be distributed to affected property owners. New York State does not do so.

An analysis by the Community Service Society of New York indicates that between the 2010 and 2020 census, West Harlem lost 3,800 Black residents and 4,500 Latinx residents. The report also notes that the share of Community District 9's private rental housing stock that is rent regulated decreased from 65% in 2008 to 48% in 2022, a loss of nearly 6,000 regulated rentals.[13]

In 2007, Columbia students launched a 10-day hunger strike focused on the university's planned Manhattanville expansion, arguing that "Columbia needs to take eminent domain off the table for the commercial property-owners in the area and reach agreements with them on an individual basis." Yet as Shoemaker writes, the university did eventually invoke eminent domain with the support of local and state officials, and in this case "'public use' was considered by the court to be both economic development and the educational and community benefits that come with the expansion of an institution of higher education."[14] Shoemaker argues that "just compensation" nearly always "undercompensates the homeowner" by focusing on "fair market price" rather than a parcel's current, actual value. But to Columbia's credit, they ultimately negotiated voluntarily with all but two private property owners, reaching private deals with all of them on an ad hoc, negotiated basis. After multiple rounds of negotiations over the course of years, the two property owners who refused to accept Columbia's offer were Gurnam Singh, whose family owned and operated two gas stations on 125th Street, and Nicholas Sprayregen, who owned four buildings and a "Tuck-It-Away" moving and storage business. Both of these property owners ultimately received just compensation through eminent domain, in a move that most likely gave them far less money than a voluntary agreement with Columbia would have provided.[15] Both Mr. Singh and his wife, Ms. Kauer, who spent near twenty-five years building their gas stations, said that Columbia had threatened them and both had sustained stress-related physical injuries from the experience. They said that Columbia had offered them $1 million to relocate to a site in Jackson Heights, Queens, where they were worried they would receive far less business. Additionally, Singh had personal reservations about owning another gas station in Queens after his brother was fatally shot while working at a different Queens gas station during an armed robbery.

Ultimately, Sprayregen and Singh did not negotiate individually with Columbia and the Empire State Development Corporation invoked eminent domain on the sites. The project was determined to be a public use and the full 17-acre area was cleared for the university, set to house new sciences, art, and business schools, as well as administrative and mixed-use facilities. Sprayregen and council filed a lawsuit that was dismissed by the New York State Supreme Court, which argued that the City Planning Department needed only to show a "rational basis" for the planned possessory takings of their parcels.[16]

As part of the possessory takings process for Manhattanville, as well as the West Harlem Rezoning and Academic Mixed-Use Development schemes proposed by the university and the Department of City Planning (DCP), the university went through both the city-mandated Uniform Land Use Review Procedure (ULURP) and drafted an Environmental Impact Statement (EIS) for the project.[17] Both processes include a mandated set of procedural due process requirements, including public comments. These public processes also involved engaging with Community Board 9's alternative 197-a Plan, which was drafted by community organizations as another, community-based planning vision for the neighborhood. Commentors in public meetings ranged from community members (The Harlem Tenants Council, individual residents, WeACT [a West Harlem environmental justice advocacy group],[18] a local chapter of the National Association for the Advancement of Colored People, the Mirabal Sisters Cultural and Community Center, and many more) to other civic stakeholders ranging from the American Institute of Architects to the Air Resources Group. Private developers and consultants connected to the project also weighed in, as did stakeholders, alumni of Columbia, and interested residents from as far away as Texas. Public comments to the proposal, available through the NYC City Planning Department's Environmental Impact Statement draft, each received dedicated responses from the City and DCP.[19] For example, a common argument was that "The CPC [City Planning Commission] public hearing was closed off to the people of Harlem. There would have been a full audience if it was held on 125th Street at the State Building."[20] DCP stakeholders responded that the combined ULURP and EIS process meetings met the city's required standard of a public hearing, and the associated procedural due process requirements. DCP argued that numerous public-hearing and procedural due process requirements were held throughout 2007. Another comment argued that members of the public were not properly notified of the hearings, to which DCP responded that We ACT was not registered appropriately as an "interested party" and that there were no procedural due process violations.[21] Some comments were positive reflections of the Manhattanville campus process and its community and environmental impact. Select comments sought to make constructive changes on the margins of the existing project. But most community comments were critical, and raised concerns about both the project itself and the city procedures of its implementation and approval. Well past project implementation, community groups continue to resist and oppose the project altogether, while others rally to hold Columbia to account on statutorily mandated promises from the CBA. For example, during Juneteenth of 2024, dozens of politicians, community advocates, residents, and Columbia students gathered to reflect on university incursions to date, and sought to support a New York State Senate Bill (no. 9028), which would halt all future expansion by Columbia University into Harlem.

An Alternative Plan

The New York City charter specifies that, under Section 197-a, community boards may come together and generate plans for land use and urban development of areas within their community board areas. These plans are then reviewed and examined by the City Planning Commission. Manhattan's Community Board 9 (CB-9) chose to do just this, publishing a 197-a plan for the area of Manhattanville located within the community board's jurisdiction.[22] Notably, CB-9 borders begin at 110th street and run all the way to 155th street in Manhattan, bordered on the west by the Hudson River and on the east by Manhattan Avenue, Morningside Avenue, and then St. Nicholas Avenue. Accordingly, many Columbia

University students, faculty, and other affiliates live within CB-9 borders. In planning law courses, for multiple years there has been an experiential learning assignment where students are asked to attend, observe, and reflect on a city planning process, with students keeping legal issues related to planning in mind. Many students choose to attend a local meeting of their community board, which in many cases is CB-9.

After Columbia University's Manhattanville master plan was released and publicized in 2003, the community board met extensively to discuss the plan, its potential implications, and courses of action in response. Key civil society institutions within the area were also heavily involved in engaging and interpreting the plan: West Harlem Environmental Action, Inc. (WE ACT for Environmental Justice) was one such key stakeholder, as was the office of U.S. Congressman Charles Rangel, who served in Congress until 2017. They submitted their 197-a alternative plan to the City's Department of City Planning (DCP) in August 2005, and submitted a revised version in November 2007.[23]

WE ACT, led by Peggy Shepherd, foregrounded potential concerns of displacement and gentrification, and responded with possibilities for anti-displacement and equitable development in Manhattanville. Writing in a 2005 publication, "The Time Has Come," WE ACT noted concerns about Manhattanville: "The goal of WE ACT's Sustainable Development program is to develop and apply tools that empower the residents of Northern Manhattan to plan, design and achieve a healthy, sustainable and environmentally just community," including "organizing residents and environmental groups to ensure that Columbia University's planned expansion of its Harlem campus into Manhattanville has a positive impact on both the environment and public health."[24]

The publication notes that WE ACT had worked with individual faculty and academic programs at Columbia successfully, and did not oppose development in Manhattanville altogether; however, they registered concerns about participation and community voice. The publication also noted that, "In the first half of 2005 alone, the New York Metropolitan Transportation Authority tried to renege on an agreement reached 5 years ago. The Mayor and the City Council attempted to reopen and expand a marine transfer station sited in Harlem. Columbia University continued its refusal to engage seriously in dialog around its plans for a huge expansion into Manhattanville in West Harlem. Each of these is yet another expression of injustice—whether intended or not."[25] Put simply, WE ACT's frustrations were both substantive and procedural: they felt ignored by Columbia University, shut out of a planning process that would significantly affect a neighborhood in which WE ACT was, and is, deeply embedded.

With WE ACT and other Manhattan CB-9 stakeholders frustrated by the university, an alterative plan crystalized. Notes Manhattan CB-9 in their overall framing of the plan: "Recommendations include preservation of the historic neighborhoods of Morningside and Hamilton Heights and a special mixed-use district for Manhattanville. Other priorities are affordable housing, preservation of industrial jobs, and improved environmental quality." The full plan neatly compares Columbia University's proposal with their alternative.[26] Compared with Columbia's Proposal, the 197-a plan is both more incremental and contextual in nature, and more community-focused. Top goals of the plan, for example, include that the city "mandate affordable housing in the district, preserve existing affordable housing, and increase the number of housing opportunities for low, moderate- and middle income residents, including seniors" and "identify sites for new public schools and explore strategies to improve services for aged and young people, including consideration of the feasibility of providing multigenerational arts and cultural facilities," among other recommendations.[27]

A special zoning designation for the district would allow for the continuation of light manufacturing uses in the area, as well as public access to a new waterfront park along the Hudson River.[28] Notably, because many of the parcels were by 2005 and 2007 already acquired by Columbia University through private negotiations, the 197-a plan did not shy away from the existence of a Manhattanville campus. Rather, they sought to eschew the university-led comprehensive planning approach with what instead amounted to a contextual, community-driven approach, one prioritizing affordable housing, the waterfront park, and light manufacturing with associated employment benefits.[29] Upon further revisions, 197-a did not envision the Columbia facilities as a full-scale "campus" but rather as an integrated set of university facilities alongside housing and industrial parcels.

In response to the Manhattan CB-9 alternative plan, DCP crafted a legally mandated "impact analysis," comparing key aspects of both plans against one another. DCP argued, in a standard impact analysis, that the "197-a Plan Alternative 1 would result in no significant adverse impacts on land use, zoning, and public policy. However, the two proposals would result in different land use patterns and densities."[30] The impact analysis considered factors like noise, construction levels, travel demand, and air quality. In Appendix N.2, DCP provides quantitative tabulations of relevant considerations, analyzing the university's plan and the 197-a alternative side by side.[31] Given that neither plan would result in "adverse impacts" of an environmental nature, or with regard to land-use and urban development, DCP was free to endorse the proposed plan, Columbia's Manhattanville campus.

Community Benefits Agreement (CBA)

With community members and civil society organizations unable to further advance their alternative plan, they sought instead to use power of *presence*—organizing, moral suasion, and sentiment on campus—to influence the university to incorporate key community provisions into the proposal currently being implemented. Students' 2007 on-campus hunger strike served as an important call to the university that students on its campus recognized the West Harlem community demands as connected to broader issues of social and environmental justice.[32] Columbia had committed over $6.3 billion to the new campus, and would receive over $172 million annually in tax breaks on properties, in light of the university's nonprofit status. Accordingly, savvy community leaders recognized the possibility for a negotiated community benefits agreement related to the campus, and ultimately secured one in 2009 for a remarkable amount of money: $150 million.

Although the CBA was passed in 2009, protestors worked to ensure Columbia would honor its commitment (Mihali, 2011).

Dorsey argues that "While opponents [of the Manhattanville campus expansion] were unable to prevent the expansion or change it in the ways they had hoped," they were successful in securing the CBA.[33] CBAs, Dorsey continues, can be defined as "contractual agreements between represented community groups and developers that detail specific benefits a developer will provide to the community in exchange for public support of the proposed project." In the case of the Manhattanville CBA, the West Harlem Community Benefits Agreement of 2009 was signed along with the West Harlem Local Development Corporation (WHLDC), itself an offshoot of Manhattan CB9. The CBA required Columbia work with WHLDC on a suite of initiatives, including but not limited to:

- A $76 million fund with annual grants for workforce development, education, historic preservation, the arts, and community facilities;
- a $20 million affordable housing fund, also administered by WHLDC, with $4 million set aside specifically for legal expenses;
- a $30 million K-5 public Teachers College Community School, which opened in 2011; and
- a $20 million commitment for local resident access to in-kind university services, such as Manhattanville campus amenities and businesses, for 25 years.[34]

Columbia University also reports on their honoring of the CBA, and submits reports to WHLDC annually as part of its "implementation plan" to ensure promises are being kept.[35]

The CBA's implementation was slow to begin. For one, WHLDC was originally a smaller-capacity organization, and stewarding hundreds of millions of dollars required a new level of institutional capacity. Indeed, the organization originally lacked an office space and dispensed only a small amount of grant money in its first three years of operation.[36] However, WHLDC eventually met annual spending targets, and Columbia began to honor its end of the CBA as well, with students diligently watching.

The CBA seeks continuity with community stakeholders, and genuine partnership with Columbia University. The Plan's preamble proceeds as follows: "CU has acknowledged its intent to collaborate with the Local Community, and in response, the elected officials, community, civic and business leaders in West Harlem formed the WHLDC pursuant to the N.Y. Not-For-Profit Corporation Law §1411 (McKinney 2005) in order to negotiate and implement this CBA with CU, which describes the manner in which the Local Community will share in the economic, educational, cultural, environmental and social benefits associated with CU's Manhattanville Project, in the spirit of the guiding principles set forth in CB 9's 197-a Plan, to the extent the same does not conflict with CU's obligations set forth in the Governing Documents."[37] Contributions from Columbia, including the benefits fund, the affordable housing fund, and in-kind facilities and services benefits, were all registered with New York City officials (like the comptroller's office) and the university was required to keep detailed annual records.[38] Some provisions of the CBA were small but could theoretically play an important legal role well into the future: for example, Columbia was required not to support any effort that might involve privatization of public housing owned by the New York City Housing Authority (NYCHA).[39] Similarly, the university was required to make a good faith commitment toward workforce development and minority, women, and low-income workers for the project.[40]

Columbia, as well as WHLDC, touted the CBA agreement as a landmark victory, and a novel approach to doing equitable urban development. Paul, however, writing for the progressive publication *Planners Network*, came to the opposite conclusion.[41] Writing how the CBA showed that there was a "need for reform in New York City planning," Paul argued that "undemocratic appointed bodies like the City Planning Commission and Empire State Development Corporation are endowed with extraordinary powers while community boards are mere advisory bodies," which enabled Columbia University to *manipulate* the planning process and local democracy more broadly. The CBA, argued Paul, was merely the best the West Harlem community could do in a structural context where "the lack of accountability and transparency effectively filters democracy out of the decision-making process to the advantage of those with economic and political power." Paul's perspectives are echoed by New York City Council member Tony Avella, who argued that Columbia never seriously changed or even reconsidered its original 2003 plan, perhaps even building in or planning for the CBA from the start.

Critics of the CBA approach argue instead for a holistic, and indeed democratic, approach to the planning process in New York, and above all one that acknowledges differences in social and economic power. Such a lens is *precisely* aligned with the curricular goals of Columbia GSAPP's own urban planning program. Yet Columbia GSAPP faculty and administration played multiple roles in the Manhattanville campus expansion project themselves, including supporting the CBA.

The Role of Columbia GSAPP

Despite its critical academic posture to the Manhattanville project and the negotiated CBA, Columbia GSAPP was actually included within the university's "community engagement work" to mollify residents. This occurred through regular "community-based courses," which often featured student projects working in and with West Harlem partners, and eventually through the appointment of Professor Maxine Griffith as Senior Advisor to the University President.[42] Griffith, born in Harlem and a prolific expert on urban and regional planning, land use and landed-property regimes, and affordable housing, was in many ways the perfect choice to lead these negotiations. Griffith's progressive planning bona fides meant she was held in high regard by progressive planning institutions and scholars; her Harlem community connections also garnered respect locally.[43]

Yet not all Columbia GSAPP affiliates supported the university and GSAPP's approach to the CBA. Pacheco, for example, examined an effort by Black GSAPP faculty and students to push for more "comprehensive reforms" around university efforts.[44] Some of these proposed reforms were internal to university programs and processes, for example with a call to "engage in the hard work of unlearning white supremacy," and "understanding anti-black racism through a deep analysis and investigation of whiteness and white supremacy" within GSAPP curricula. But others looked outward, and specifically to Harlem. For example, calls for "initiated community-based design and planning studios that worked with Harlem residents and organizations" sought to advance partnerships in the spirit of former GSAPP colleague Dr. Sharon Sutton. Another recommendation was for the university to "critically engage and exchange with Black communities, scholars, and makers" and "recognize, engage, and establish forms of exchange with Black communities beyond GSAPP; foremost engaging the surrounding context of Columbia University, including Harlem and the Spitzer School of Architecture at City College, as well as HBCUs, the Caribbean, and the African continent for recruitment, participatory justice initiatives, along with scholarly and creative projects and programming," sought to advance more equitable and co-generated knowledge. The letter, circulated and endorsed by Black GSAPP faculty members in the wake of the 2020 racial reckoning after the murder of George Floyd, was written by eight Black faculty members: Amina Blacksher, Lance Freeman, Mario Gooden, Jerome Haferd, Malo Hutson, Gordon Kipping, Justin Garrett Moore, and Mabel Wilson. Its tone reflects an attitude held by GSAPP minority faculty that the university's longstanding approach to planning was white supremacist and deeply disconnected from nearby community injustices. In reading the letter, outrage is palpable.[45] Faculty outrage seemed to center on the fact that Columbia did not negotiate with West Harlem community members in good faith, including through the Columbia Manhattanville CBA. Yet perhaps because of the role of senior faculty members like Prof. Griffith, the CBA was never called out explicitly, nor was the university's troubling dispossession of Manhattanville residents.

Moreover, throughout Columbia's process of proposing and now implementing the Manhattanville project, Columbia GSAPP students and faculty have been active in community-based efforts of resistance. Throughout, some of the *best* grassroots journalistic reporting of the violences of displacement were conducted by student-journalists at *The Columbia Spectator* and other college newspapers like the *Yale Daily News*.[46] With the *Spectator*, the very name of the paper speaks to a troubling, longstanding lack of agency between students and faculty, versus administrative leaders at Columbia.

Therefore, Columbia GSAPP students, faculty, and administrators have ambiguous and at times multi-faceted connections to the Manhattanville campus project. Many began their intellectual work in planning unsure about the project, and some went on to work on studio courses or practicum courses furthering university goals. Others, through critical academic courses or student-run clubs or journal publications, interrogated the project, met and interviewed community members, or participated in protests or rallies to seek an end to (or changes to) the university's approach. In the section that follows, I foreground the planning law classroom as one case study of this very duality present at Columbia GSAPP. As the course's critical theoretic frame and pedagogical approach encounter the practical campus context of Columbia University within Harlem, student insights, I found, were particularly generative. Such insights may hold relevance to the field of progressive planning more broadly.

3
TEACHING MANHATTANVILLE AT COLUMBIA

As the previous sections have outlined, Columbia GSAPP played a major role in envisioning, planning, and implementing Columbia's campus expansion plan between 2003 and the present. Yet the institution is also deeply and genuinely committed to critical pedagogy, social justice, and planning praxis that reckons with historical and contemporary injustice. In this section, I outline my approach to engaging Manhattanville over the course of four years serving as a recitation section leader and Teaching Assistant (TA) for the Planning Law course, and consider student engagements and reactions as well. Here, I critically reflect on what it means to teach Planning Law—and in particular possessory and regulatory takings—in this setting.

Classroom Engagements

I TA-ed Planning Law every Spring between 2021 and 2024. The instructor of record has changed and so, too, have members of the full-class teaching team. Accordingly, I have seen different approaches to the course over time, engaging distinct casebooks and course materials.[1] Regardless, I usually spend at least two class sessions on eminent domain and both possessory and regulatory takings. In the past two years, I spent three dedicated class sessions on this topic. It is also very common for students to discuss this topic in particular through their own written assignments, and even in their final assignments. When teaching Planning Law, I inevitably engage the example of Manhattanville: students are familiar with the context coming into class, and are able to apply legal insights to this example.

When teaching possessory and regulatory takings in Planning Law, I open with a conceptual overview common in most casebooks and legal approaches to the topic. This includes, as mentioned earlier, clarifying the difference between possessory takings as the physical occupation of a parcel of property, typically by a governmental entity (or in the public interest); and regulatory takings that focus on challenges to local regulations that "go too far" and reduce the economic value of a given parcel of land. I also advance different legal arguments that have been used to assess takings, historically and in the present. These include the legal argument that local regulations do not "substantially advance" a public interest, or "totally deprive" a property of its value, constituting a de facto taking. Engaging *Penn Central*,[2] I also discuss the "multi-factor balancing test" as a way to assess takings, and engage the factors that planners and courts might weigh.

During the course of this overview, I discuss how the Fifth Amendment to the U.S. Constitution also requires compensation for *temporary* regulatory takings, and moratoria. Regulatory takings, whether permanent or temporary, require compensation if the said regulation prohibits any practical use of the property.[3] However, moratoria are not per se "takings" because they do not deprive property owners of *all* economic value of their land (including potential value); property owners experience no more than a "pause" in the value of their land.[4] Finally, I discuss *Lucas v South Carolina* (1992), which is a generative case about "shifting sands" in coastal South Carolina property claims, given that the case has relevance for climate change and planning adaptation, and because it underscores the U.S. Supreme Court's more conservative turn toward limiting the ability of local governments to regulate private property over time. Throughout these topical engagements, I solicit student discussions in class.

Discussions over takings in my Planning Law course involve what might best be described as Socratic dialectic: on the one hand, eminent domain is one of the most important ways in which the local state, a democratic and *public* body, can shape the form and use of land even when private landowners have claim to it. This is essential for the construction of any large-scale public project, from roads to bridges to public amenities like parks. In this context, we discuss "the holdout problem"[5] and how a patchwork of private landowners makes building large-scale public projects like subways or public sidewalks difficult, time-consuming, and costly.

On the other hand, students typically bring up how the practical effects of eminent domain often favor wealthy, privileged residents of a city or community over low-income people and people of color. To this end, eminent domain often ends up displacing or dispossessing residents long marginalized by the state in favor of "public" projects that benefit wealthier residents. A classic example of such a project, from New York, is Robert Moses' Cross-Bronx

Expressway, discussed in Caro's *Power Broker*.[6] Here, low-income residents of the Bronx's East Tremont neighborhood are displaced in preference for a highway that prioritizes the needs and conveniences of suburban residents and economic growth, and Moses even worked to ensure that many of his parkways were built with low bridges so that only private cars, and not public busses, could travel there.[7]

In this context, we consider Manhattanville. Some students note that the existing West Harlem land uses were under-utilized, especially the area's light industrial parcels. Others counter with the *residential* displacement that was necessary for Manhattanville to occur. Some students bring up the issue of voluntary settlement and private negotiation between Columbia and landowners, while others invoke the eminent domain—limited in scope—that did occur. The discussion inevitably historicizes the project: the 1968 proposal for the Columbia gym in Harlem and the slow, steady displacement of residents between 120th and 123rd street as part of North Campus over the 1970s and 1980s.

In 2022, a student successfully argued in class that community voice was adequately reflected in the 50-page Community Benefits Agreement (CBA), which kept many Manhattanville spaces on the ground floor of new campus buildings open to the public.[8] Indeed, she argued, an accessible and welcoming coffee shop at the Forum, and relevant community theatre programming at the Lenfest Center, might both be of more neighborhood benefit to locals than a gas station, car repair shop, or private residents. In 2023 and 2024, however, students vehemently disagreed with those assumptions: while the Forum and Lenfest spaces might nominally be "public," they do not *feel* public or welcoming to local residents, argued a student in 2024. And indeed, the built environment of these "public" spaces is designed to feel austere and unwelcoming at the ground floor level. It would be remarkable if any local residents used the spaces and felt comfortable doing so.

With these engagements in mind, in Spring 2024 I held a Planning Law course session in situ at Manhattanville for a walk-about.

In situ engagements

These in situ engagements with Planning Law occurred on February 19 and April 1, 2024. Visual highlights from the trips are reproduced below. Figures highlight some of the major buildings and spaces of the Manhattanville campus in its current stage of implementation. Figures also take a deep dive into the question of "public amenities" and the accessibility of both nominally public outdoor spaces and nominally public ground-floor indoor spaces. Finally, figures reveal student engagements.

Classroom Discussions and Reflections

In addition to the in situ engagements with Manhattanville, on April 8 I held space within the Planning Law class for a critical discussion about Manhattanville and students' observations. The following questions guided discussion, which lasted about 20 minutes:

1. Does the neighborhood around Manhattanville seem "blighted"?
2. Does the Manhattanville campus seem to be serving a "public purpose"?

The Manhattanville walkthroughs. Walkthroughs reveal a campus that remains under construction. However, students pointed out the stark contrast between the glass high-rises of Manhattanville and the public housing projects surrounding it. For example, the large complex at 3333 Broadway (top right, right side) was once part of the Mitchell-Lama housing program but was privatized in 2015. Also of note is an extensive private security presence (bottom left) and signage touting public amenities like wi-fi and wheelchair accessibility (bottom right). (All images by author, 2024.)

Student experiences of Manhattanville. Students felt that public spaces and ground-floor spaces were only nominally inclusive. Students felt the area to be somewhat austere and unwelcoming. In some cases, as with the Columbia Business School building, there was no public access whatsoever (see photo top left). Public outdoor spaces had minimal urban design interventions or urban "furniture" that would welcome locals, or for that matter residents of the Columbia campus community. (All images by author, 2024.)

Public Amenities? While the plaza at left was expressly included in the Community Benefits Agreement (CBA) as a "public plaza," it had no users on both February 19 and April 1, during visits on both cold winter and warm spring days. Likewise, the large plaza near the Lenfest Center sat empty in April, as did the bike racks around which the façade was designed. At bottom left, a sign mandated by the CBA and New York City's Privately Operated Public Spaces (POPS) program designates the space as public and open 24 hours per day. (All images by author, 2024.)

Public Amenities: One exception to the concern over public and community use is the "Dear Mama" coffee shop, located in the Jerome L. Greene Science Center at 611 W 129th St. as part of the Manhattanville campus. The coffee shop was well-used by students and locals alike, and flyers and community advertisements discussed local events and meetings. While students found the coffee shop to be a well-used, public, and democratic space, other spaces, like the VITAL Climbing Gym, in West Harlem in The Forum at 3225 Broadway, were found to be more exclusionary in their clientele. Students noted that some of the most well-used spaces were small, interstitial zones for workers, including the lunch cart in the figure in the bottom right, 125th street and Broadway. (All images by author, 2024.)

Select members of my Planning Law course section during an in situ walkabout April 1, 2024. (Image by author, 2024.)

3. Does it seem that the project either benefits the surrounding community directly (i.e. with public space) or provides indirect community benefits (jobs, economic development, or an increase in property values)?

4. By way of the takings process, we've discussed how the university negotiated a $76 million Community Benefits Agreement with the West Harlem community. Do you see any evidence of those negotiations?

Students discussed the subjective nature of "blight," and the racialized nature of the term. Such a freighted meaning of "blight" is by no means unique to Manhattanville: indeed, the original employment of the label in *Berman v. Parker*[9] speaks to a similarly suspect use case. Students also noted where industrial spaces with historic value—such as the Columbia University Studebaker Building at 615 W 131st St.—have been maintained and preserved, albeit for new (university) purposes.

Students also discussed the seemingly "public" nature of the project and its benefits. There is no doubt, many students argued, that the campus stands out in contrast to neighboring buildings, and especially the higher-density public and formerly public housing units surrounding the new campus. The widespread use of private security roaming officers, private Columbia University security vehicles, and security cameras was also something students astutely noticed, and something I had initially missed in my earlier forays to campus. The public spaces were indeed present, as legally specified in the CBA and in Columbia POPS documentation, but were not themselves well or widely used. It is possible that with construction ongoing, and with street trees and urban furniture still incomplete, the observations in winter and spring 2024 are premature. However, the spaces did not feel welcoming or inviting to the class, and the suspicious lack of public amenities in the middle of key plazas—for example in front of Lenfest Center and the Jerome Greene Science Center—further puzzled students. "The Plaza," an amenity negotiated in the CBA, was completely vacant during both visits. Moreover, there were no visible public-space connections to the Hudson River waterfront, a point conveyed expressly in the Community Board 197-a alternative plan that the Manhattanville campus plan does not yet seem to have addressed.

A bright spot noticed by students, however, was, again, the Dear Mama Coffee Shop, located in the Jerome Greene Science Center on 129th St. Although it is a private business, it seemed well-used by locals and Columbia affiliates alike. Moreover, surrounding the coffee shop there is a dedicated ground-floor public space and community center with wi-fi, workspaces, and comfortable tables. The class noticed locals working on laptops or having meetups.

In contrast, students were less impressed by the publicness of the Lenfest Center, even though the site has a museum and gallery space. It is possible that the Lenfest space, as per the terms of the CBA, is better activated during public shows or performances with local community relevance, or when local artists' work is being showcased. The Forum and its ground-floor climbing gym also seemed well-used, though the class was divided about its publicness: some saw it as exclusionary and a harbinger of gentrification, contrasting with neighboring buildings and uses. Others saw it as a creative, needed public space intervention.

In short, students were able to engage Manhattanville's project with nuance, empirical observation, and criticality, consider the takings process alongside the current uses of the neighborhood. Throughout, there was a discussion of those who were not part of the production of space of either the campus expansion plan or the private properties that proceeded it: non-elite residents who did not own property (renters), and those who were not a part of select civic or advocacy organizations. Normatively, some students saw the CBA that emerged as a "best possible outcome" given the circumstances, and saw in Manhattanville a precedent model for community engagement in different settings nationwide. Yet others saw Manhattanville as a case of institutional paradox: Columbia's academic mission of open, critical, inclusive teaching and research lies in stark contrast to actually existing university practices just blocks away from our classroom. The heart of the problem—in Manhattanville and in countless other university-led redevelopment projects—is the link between undemocratic planning processes (ignoring the voice and sustained protests of resident renters and students alike) and unjust planning outcomes (the Manhattanville Project and its displacement of residents and destruction of community). Even as Columbia University students learn about ways to be justice-oriented and critical, their institutions actively model unjust ways of being, and of planning.

4
RESISTANT MEMORY: A CONCLUSION

Having now discussed and contextualized urban planning curricula and standards through the discipline's Planning Accreditation Board (PAB), Columbia University's social justice and critical approach to urban planning, and the background and history of the university's own urban development practices in general and with the Manhattanville project in particular, we can now ask, what does it mean to teach planning law in this setting, at Columbia's GSAPP? For me, for my students, for scholars at Columbia GSAPP and in planning more broadly, and for members of the public?

In the contemporary context of Columbia University's now in-progress Manhattanville project, I have also arrived at a question about the purpose of this book project. After all, the project plan is being implemented, and dispossession has occurred. What use it is to critically document this university-driven resident dispossession? I have arrived at the importance of mnemonic practices: remembering *what* was previously there in Manhattanville, and remembering *who* lived there and how. These mnemonic practices must also foreground those who were not displaced, but who witnessed their neighborhood and social and civic context transform.

For many locals, Manhattanville meant a loss of housing. For others, it meant a loss of a business, in some cases decades-old institutions. And for others, including Columbia affiliates, it meant a loss of community. For those still living in Manhattanville, Columbia's project might signify the start or continuation of a sort of "time lapse": residents find themselves in some kind of "state of waiting," perhaps for their own displacement, or in waiting for some degree of restitution or repair that may or may not come.

To aid in my reflexive process, I have sought to deliberately consider multiple perspectives. It is worth noting that Manhattanville as a project has substantial effects and considerable ambiguous ones, on the West Harlem community and beyond. It is also worth noting that I am originally from Colorado and attended Columbia as a graduate student; I do not have particularly intimate familial or personal ties to the neighborhood, and many others do. And from what I gather, even *within* the West Harlem community, there are passionate debates about the project: some residents and leaders see the project as an admirable way to "clean up" and add value to a portion of West Harlem complete with public spaces, community access on the ground floor of buildings, and potential future links to the Hudson River waterfront. Others are far more skeptical: the project exists as an historical continuity. It is merely the latest community incursion by Columbia in an institutional history that has involved serial dispossession: residents in Harlem, from 122nd to 125th Street, and across upper Manhattan have been battling displacement at various scales for decades, and any benefits are solely the result of community struggles and fights. Columbia is not an altruistic actor.

Such context has animated twentieth century urban planning history. Universities, nationwide, are complicit. Given that I am originally from Colorado, we might look inward. In the Denver context, low-income Latinx residents of the Auraria Neighborhood in Denver were displaced en masse in an area that is now part of the shared Auraria Higher Education Campus, a 150-acre urban campus that hosts three higher education institutions: University of Colorado Denver, Community College of Denver, and Metropolitan State University. On the Auraria Campus, CU Denver hosts the University of Colorado (CU) Denver Urban Planning Program, among other programs. Far away, in Cape Town South Africa, the famed mixed-race District Six neighborhood was razed to the ground between 1966 and 1970 by the apartheid state to make room for the Cape Peninsula University of Technology (CPUT), among other uses. Columbia's incursions are far from unique.[1]

Also concerning from an urban planning perspective is the palpable tension and animosity that exists between Columbia and the surrounding neighborhoods of Harlem. The Morningside Heights neighborhood, the setting of Columbia's current main campus, is itself an onomastic construction employed by Columbia to differentiate the neighborhood from Harlem, and there is currently an active effort to do the same with the "new" neighborhood of SoHa, or "South of Harlem."[2] Such tensions, however, are also not unique to Columbia. Yale and its relationship to New Haven, Connecticut, the University of Pennsylvania and its relationship to West Philadelphia, and the University of Chicago and its relationship to Chicago's South Side all come to mind as analogous campus/community settings with tense and unequal dynamics of place and planning.

Injustices surrounding Manhattanville operate on multiple district levels: on one level is a violence of physical dispossession and spatial incursion. Whether through pressured voluntary negotiations or through physical takings (eminent domain), Columbia has expanded into former minority neighborhoods, and Manhattanville's campus is the latest such community expansion. Alongside it, there is an epistemic and discursive injustice: Columbia denying the presence and history of the communities and residents it displaces. As Junker has carefully documented, ordinary residents and Columbia libraries have carefully archived community presence and resistance across the twentieth century.[3] For the university to claim that Manhattanville was no more than a set of little-used industrial lots is not only disingenuous, but in direct contrast to an existing archival record. Moreover, the university's narrative constitutes an erasure of the West Harlem community that makes any frank assessment or appraisal of the university's actions difficult.

American studies scholar Davarian Baldwin has documented the systemic nature of university-driven dispossession, which has occurred along lines of racial exclusion for centuries.[4] Baldwin has explored the University of Chicago's incursions into the South Side of Chicago, the city of New Haven's austerity politics amid a "transformation" of New Haven, Connecticut, and other diverse cases of "UniverCities," including campus-adjacent neighborhoods at the University of Pittsburgh (Pitt), Carnegie Mellon, Saint Louis University (SLU), New York University (NYU), George Washington University, and more.[5] A lesson emerges from Baldwin's work: universities today are vast institutions that contain within them real estate holders, private security agents, elite brokers, and administrative managers. Universities' emphases on teaching and learning can at times feel like an afterthought.

In the contexts of Auraria and District Six, marginalized communities have been displaced to make way for university campuses, but community-based institutions have helped save stories and memories of what was displaced. The History Colorado "Museum of Memory" documents "The Displaced Aurarians"; the "I am Auraria" exhibition on display at the Auraria Library features photos, oral histories, and artifacts from residents; a community mural was organized for the Plaza building in the heart of the Auraria Higher Education Center, increasing awareness of this history; and a database and map of the Auraria neighborhood and its residents between 1955 and 1973 is being digitally created by partners at CU Denver, including planners.[6] The oral histories bear witness and save a record of what was once there, from residents' perspectives, and feature residents with dignity. In one oral history, former resident Sheila Perez-Kindle said, "It was just a good place to live. It was comfortable, it was home, you know, to a lot of people."[7] Reflecting later on returning to Auraria years after dispossession, she remarked: "I felt like we were not welcome on the campus."[8] An oral history of Greg and Rita Gomez-Delgado involved similar themes. They discussed life on 9th Street in Auraria: "I miss most of all the safety of walking . . . being able to walk the streets without worrying about, are they [my children] coming home? Because we used to walk from 9th Street and we would walk all the way downtown, around downtown, and then go to Woolworth's and buy our pizza, and walk on home. And our parents never really worried about us because there was nothing really to worry about: every house was a relative."[9] From the voice and perspective of these and other community storytellers, the project explores the history of a diverse and tight-knit community, and speaks to the tearing apart of that community for urban renewal and the Auraria higher education project.

In District Six, South Africa, the community District Six Museum[10] features tour guides and docents who are formerly displaced neighborhood residents. The museum furthers a South African "flourishing, contested, culture of memory" in South Africa and of apartheid.[11] Residents "re-work the past in terms of the present in order to establish divergence,"[12] and in so doing may romanticize the neighborhood's past in order to agentically comment on their removal by powerful institutions. Like Auraria, in other words, District Six was never perfect. Yet with both District Six and Auraria, the neighborhood's histories are preserved through community narrative work that contests official narratives of "blight" and "highest and best use"— languages that are hegemonic in urban planning and planning law.

Mnemonic practices and systematic documentation are essential forms of resistance, whether in Cape Town, South Africa's District Six, Denver's Auraria neighborhood, or in West Harlem near Columbia. If locals start to remember, that process entails making connections with the communities that have been oppressed and locked out of urban development decision-making. The process of remembering is a process of not just contesting, but of re-connecting and re-building. Memories serve as an imperfect way to re-building communities that are supposedly already dispersed. The case of Manhattanville may even inspire a redefinition of memory itself, how we process memory, and how we collectively memorialize and archive. Collective memory becomes a question of how residents might build and maintain an archive, and how that archive in turn serves as a foundation for oppositional consciousness and community-building within the spatial container of universities' vision.[13] After all, many residents remain on the proverbial doorsteps of these institutions, and many are employed by these universities, often as essential caretakers committed to the educational mission that enables them to function.

These liminal spaces—of individual and collective memory, of oppositional consciousness, and of presence both historically fixed and continuously felt—can cultivate revolutionary spaces. They can also fertilize local soil and arm locals with knowledge for when the next, too often violent, institutional incursion inevitably arrives.

Far beyond Columbia, the discipline of urban planning is intimately familiar with practices of dispossession for a "highest and best use"—from highway building to contemporary projects like that in Manhattanville. The fact that universities are advancing such projects raises an important, globally relevant, corollary question: what *work,* if any, is criticality doing in these academic spaces?

In the field of urban planning, planners hosting participatory visioning sessions that "check a box" and "mollify residents" is an increasingly common practice.[14] But are social-justice planning programs at elite universities doing no more than making planners better at mollifying community residents? Are planners steeped in social justice pedagogy playing roles that assuage communities that planners "understand their concerns," "have their backs," and "genuinely care?" Without power to shape the rules and processes of urban development, criticality may raise important issues and concerns, and even create alliances between progressive advocacy planners and community members.[15] But it may not change serial dispossession that occurs in places like Manhattanville.

Another possibility is even more sinister: does the increasing planners' criticality actually mean the local state is *less* able to coordinate and plan large-scale public projects, from large-scale public-transit projects like the California High-Speed Rail (CA HSR) to Massachusetts's Sagamore Bridge reconstruction? What importance ought we give to elements of the public-private-non-profit arrangements in projects like these?

While planners preventing displacement from public projects may avoid the kind of violent dispossession that marked mid-twentieth century highway-building, projects like the Pfizer Campus in New London (*Kelo v. City of New London*)[16] or Columbia Manhattanville reveal how elites collaborate to shape the production of space. Namely, actors across multiple sectors—public institutions, private firms, universities, and more—act in ways that are very difficult for critical and progressive planners to contest. Are municipal planners less equipped to push through projects at a regulatory level, such that private consultants and firms then do this work instead? In the wake of the National Environmental Protection Act, or NEPA, Environmental Impact Statement (EIS) consultants have emerged as a cottage industry; takings consultants have similarly emerged following cases like *Penn Central* and its multi-factor balancing test.

These thoughts raise more questions than provide answers. To teach planning law critically, at the very least, reveals the complicities of our own institutions—in this case Columbia University. Rather than focus broadly on private firms or even on universities globally, should the very first aim of critical planners at Columbia be to ensure that there is a more equitable, just planning practice within the institution of Columbia? Or is that an overly insular focus?

Campus struggles have alternately led to successes, and to failures. The Columbia campus protests in 1968 and 2024 both explicitly touched on themes related to university oppression in Harlem, with the 1968 protests taking on this theme more specifically and the 2024 protests focused on Israel and Palestine. In both cases, however, contestation at Columbia has precipitated broader activism nationwide and even globally. Might contesting institutional practices at Columbia have the potential to constitute a generative "first step" from which resistance to other unjust takings could grow?

Ultimately, in courses like Planning Law, and well beyond, faculty and students should move from critical reflections and knowledge to a type of "praxis" and phronesis, or practical wisdom, that marries progressive knowledge with action, in myriad ways. The pragmatist John Dewey was himself a theorist also deeply engaged in struggles for political change. His phrasing "democracy as a way of life" put him on the front lines of labor strikes and dangerous political battles.[17] Would such a pragmatist political approach mean teaching planning law concepts experientially, working with (or volunteering for) community groups like WeAct as critical to student learning?

Instilling an ethic and an approach where urban planners ought to be working more with community groups and civic leaders is important, but itself must be carefully designed. There are both helpful, and extractive, ways to engage community institutions, and while some approaches might benefit students and university reputations, they may harm communities or waste community leaders' time. Praxis that involves deep, reciprocal relationships is fundamental. And praxis that is solutions-oriented—focused on nascent or promising planning strategies (even promising strategies of contestation) where planners have "skin in the game" as well—may hold particular promise.

Alternatively, might there be forms of powerful, oppositional memory—what I am tentatively calling *mnemonic resistance*—that enable and create community through memory? History Colorado's work with Denver's Auraria neighborhood is an admirable example. In West Harlem (now Manhattanville), physical vestiges of the past, like a renovated Studebaker factory, remain. Or an old waterfront view. *Mnemonic resistance* can connect memories of those displaced and those still present to the larger social implications of urban planning, planning law, and university-driven dispossession.

With regard to urban planning, Columbia's Manhattanville campus expansion project has officially concluded; the project is under active implementation. Individual property owners like Gurnam Singh and Nicholas Sprayregen have unsuccessfully sued the university, and the courts have decided in the university's favor, justifying a possessory takings. Whether through voluntary settlements or by invoking eminent domain, the university has assembled the land outlined in President Bollinger's 2003 press release and statement. Civic and community institutions, like Manhattan Community Board 9 and WE ACT for Environmental Justice, remain critical to ensuring that the Community Benefits Agreement (CBA), negotiated between 2003 and 2009 and signed in 2009, is faithfully implemented.[18] And these groups as well as students will need to remain vigilant in advocating for promises made in the CBA document, such as pledges for public, accessible ground-floor indoor spaces, outdoor public spaces of gathering and meeting available to neighborhood groups, connections to the Hudson River waterfront, and local community employment and art programming at the business school and the

Lenfest Center for the Arts, respectively. Much as with Robert Moses's Cross Bronx Expressway, affected residents have left, and those who remain are already contending with a changing neighborhood and new amenities. And in that sense, the "battle" over the Manhattanville campus expansion plan is over.

With a retrospective and reflexive frame in mind, then, how ought I—as an institutionally affiliated member of the Columbia University community—inhabit these spaces. As I graduated and moved on from Columbia, I asked this rhetorical question not merely for myself, but for current and future graduate students, undergraduate students, faculty, adjunct lecturers, and staff. Are there mnemonic practices of remembering what was once there in Manhattanville? Humanistic or archival best practices on which to draw? Resident perspectives or wisdom, tied to the land and to space? Are there ways to engage those who were displaced? What about neighborhood residents who were not displaced but whose neighbors and neighborhoods have changed around them?

Laurajane Smith, in her seminal book *Uses of Heritage*, considers concepts of "authorized cultural heritage" and "subaltern or dissenting heritage discourses" in her argument that the significance of heritage as a concept depends on constructed social and cultural values in the present day.[19] Following Smith's insights, which foreground aboriginal heritage and memory in Queensland, Australia, we might say that the stakes of remembering, and indeed the ability to remember, are not a given. Mnemonic resistance, then, is no surefire outcome from Columbia University's acts of serial displacement. Rather, residents' negotiation of a sense of place will require acts of self-reference and active memory-keeping, toward creating an alternative Authorized Heritage Discourse (AHD) about the area's history.[20] Mnemonic resistance in this context may benefit from the comparatively vast, and at times digitally held, archives of what transpired in present-day Manhattanville. An active digital paper trail by *Columbia Spectator* student journalists, for example, reveal intimate policy choices and decisions over decades. Carmelo Ignaccolo's work on mapping intangible craftsmanship in Lebanon offers a playbook for activists and mnemonic resistors seeking to challenge dominant narratives or simply retain alternatives ones.[21] In that project, Ignaccolo and colleagues developed an atlas of living heritage that documented practices and narratives often omitted from conventional urban redevelopment plans in Lebanon, disseminating it locally through on-site installations with WhatsAppcurved bots.[22]

A challenge surrounding issues of power and voice with the Manhattanville campus expansion plan—and a challenge surrounding eminent domain and takings issues nationwide in planning law—is that those most directly and viscerally affected by the production of urban space resulting from these decisions are also those with the least institutionally legitimated voice. Renters, those without legal title or claim to own the affected parcels, were nonetheless longtime dwellers, inhabitants, of these blocks of Manhattan. Yet our system of planning law does not seriously protect renters, legally or otherwise. Whether through voluntary negotiations with Columbia or through legal battles, property owners engaged the university, and perhaps at times did so on behalf of their tenants. But the structural lack of voice for this group of people, especially in a context like New York City where apartment rentals are common, harkens back to earlier twentieth-century planning projects that more often than not razed low-income and minority urban neighborhoods because of the perception that there would be less resistance there.

The changing neighborhood around Manhattanville can be felt clearly at the level of everyday life. For example, the new and increasing presence of Columbia University private security guards at street corners, a large and growing demographic shift, the new business school buildings, and now the free Columbia night shuttles only for campus ID holders collectively remake the Manhattanville neighborhood as an exclusive campus enclave, and not part of West Harlem. Even as a former Columbia University affiliate, I feel tremendous unease walking these streets knowing what was there just a few years prior.

Fullilove and Wallace use the term "serial forced displacement" to describe the "repetitive, coercive upheaval of groups . . . in American cities due to federal, state, and local government policies."[23] There is a tremendous, measurable, collective public health impact on low-income minority communities that have experienced these repetitive waves of dispossession. Members of the West Harlem community in and around present-day Manhattanville have not always lived in West Harlem: many such residents previously lived in other parts of New York City, like the Upper West Side's "San Juan Hill" neighborhood that was itself destroyed to build Lincoln Center, or displaced from other parts of Lower Manhattan.[24] Beyond that, many African American residents of Harlem fled white nationalist terrorism in the U.S. South, a set of historic processes often referred to as the Great Migration and discussed poignantly by Wilkerson.[25]

The frame of what Wilson calls "infra-structural racism" is also generative, especially in its calls for a reparative (reparations-based) set of policy and planning responses to serial examples of dispossession.[26] Wilson argues that "urbanist practices and our built environment itself" led to "place-based manifestations of racist ideology and the institutions of slavery," further noting that responses ought to be different in different municipalities and local settings. The Manhattanville campus expansion is, in its own way, connected to this history. It is a history that remains ongoing, and one where the field of urban planning and planning law are perennially complicit.

At the end of this book's Introduction, I asked how examples of urban planning interventions like the Manhattanville project, pedagogically and otherwise, might galvanize students and instructors to respond to the complicity of their very own institutions. When planning law is taught critically, the course must address this question concretely with students, and not merely look to injustices of settler-colonial landed-property arrangements in general. While it is true that numerous seizures of "real property" continue across American cities, often with fewer ancillary community benefits than what occurred with the Manhattanville project, there are a set of important lessons, and urgent actions, needed when discussing this project in a university course setting. A few insights and takeaways:

1. The critical planning law context is instructive in providing *collective humility.* While elite American universities can be bastions of progressive thought, the fact that such progressive ideas are housed within institutional and organizational arrangements actively perpetuating injustice should give scholars pause, and raise questions about the socially (un)just nature of academic work.

2. The context can be generative for *action-oriented research.* University organizations, leaders, libraries, and archives sit at the nexus of the campus classroom and office. Faculty, PhD students, researchers, and other affiliates have perhaps the most unfettered access to this information and are, in many ways, "customers" of these institutions and accordingly hold leverage

in their decision-making. That proximity and the intimate relationship provide opportunities for engaged research.

3. Although at times fleeting, *campus and community partnerships offer promising examples of solidarity.* With the Manhattanville expansion, Columbia students have been on the front lines of contestation (for example with their 2007 ten-day hunger strike over the issue). At times, Columbia students, also a part of the Manhattan Community Board 9 community, have been present at neighborhood meetings and even in drafting the 197-a alternative plan. Yet there are power imbalances and also ethical considerations with such partnerships: Columbia students' neighborhood ties are necessarily different than affected residents' ties, and commitments can be fleeting. Moreover, local communities are not monolithic and are not infrequently intensely divided: conflict over the Community Benefits Agreement, borne partly out of a realization that Columbia would build Manhattanville regardless, provides one example. Student solidarity can be most affective when there is a posture of listening and learning from community leaders, including community disagreements. Argues Song (2021), drawing on the example of the "Metro as Sanctuary" campaign, reparative planning can play an important societal role as "movement building."

4. *Criticizing university campus-expansion policies can galvanize broader social critique.* American higher education is enmeshed within a neoliberal paradigm increasingly dependent on investment returns, boards of trustees, and high tuition dollars.[27] Campus expansion plans play a role in university strategy and financing: they increase university assets (land holdings), provide for more student enrollment and as such tuition, and allow universities to further compete in a "facilities arms race" against their elite peers.[28] Criticizing

> the injustice of campus expansion plans, therefore, offers a space for a broader, institutional critique of higher education and its purposes. The extent to which universities instead might invest in (unionized) faculty and staff, or inclusive student enrollment (including of students from affected communities like West Harlem) could be connected to an alternative paradigmatic vision of the twenty-first century university, with a planning law critique at its center.

Planners can, in their own ways, engage with any and all of the takeaways noted above. They can serve as humble and reflexive students and citizens, as community-based and action-oriented researchers, as solidaristic activists, and as social critics of the university *system* writ large. Planners can also use their specific skills honed in community planning in the wake of the Manhattanville project

In Manhattanville, memories of a twenty-year-long process of displacement exist, including within myself, on that very ground. Could such memories be the fuel to structure contestation and protest against future unjust takings? Can they be productive in other ways? What would it mean for the field of planning to think about a mnemonically informed planning practice, through sites of memory (street names, memorials, monuments), enriched and legitimated planning processes (like stronger community benefits agreement), or even new laws and policies?

NOTES

Introduction

1. Ellickson, Been, Hills, and Serkin, 2020, *Land Use Controls,* 157–59.
2 Caro, 1974, *The Power Broker.* See also: Berman, 1981, *All That Is Solid Melts into Air.*
3 Charles Bagli, the *New York Times* reporter on real estate and politics, explained the 2010 judicial victory well. Bagli, "Court Upholds Columbia Campus Expansion Plan."
4 This link provides an official project overview from the university's Manhattanville master plan: https://neighbors.columbia.edu/sites/default/files/content/Manhattanville%20Campus%20Project%20Overview.pdf. See also: Kensinger, 2018, "As Columbia Moves into Manhattanville, Its Industrial Past is Erased," *NY Curbed.*
5 The American Institute of Certified Planners (AICP) provides the only nationwide, independent verification of planners' qualifications. The AICP certification process for urban plannings is run through the American Planning Association (APA) and more information is available here: https://planning.org/aicp/. More information about the ACSP's PAB Board is available here: https://www.planningaccreditationboard.org/.
6 "PAB Accreditation Standards and Criteria," 2021, *Planning Accreditation Board*, pg. 10.
7 Forsyth, 2024, "Harvard University: Currently Accredited," *Planning Accreditation Board,* https://www.planningaccreditationboard.org/harvard-university/.
8 Saghir and Sand, 2015, "What Do City Planners Need to Know? When Do They Need to Know It?" *International Journal of Social Science Studies*, 24.

9 Forsyth, 2025, "Daring to Stop: Challenging Program-Level Learning Outcome Measurement in Urban Planning Accreditation," *Journal of Planning Education and Research.*

10 Saghir and Sand, 2015: 24.

11 "The HBS Case Method," 2014, *Harvard Business School.*

12 See, for example, Frug, 2001, *City Making.*

13 See, for example, "Title 7. Planning And Land Use," 2024, California Government Code.

14 Frug, 2001, *City Making.* See also: Rusk, 2010, *Cities without Suburbs*; and Briffault, 2000, "Localism and Regionalism."

15 Rose, 2013, *Legal Foundations of Land Use Planning.*

16 Frug, Ford, and Barron, 2014, *Local Government Law, Cases and Materials.* See also: Ellickson, Been, Hills, and Serkin, 2020, *Land Use Controls.*

17 Rose, 1985, "Possession as the Origin of Property." Berger, 2006, "It's Not About the Fox," Pg. 55. See also: Dorries, 2022, "What is Planning without Property?"

18 Povinelli, 2016, *Geontologies.*

19 Tuckness, 2020, "Locke's Political Philosophy."

20 See Rose, 1985; Berger, 2006; and Dorries, 2022.

21 See Rose, 1985.

22 *Penn Central* involves the case of landmarks preservation ruling at Grand Central Station, owned by the Penn Central railroad company. After the demolition of Penn Station, New Yorkers were outraged to have lost a beautiful station to midcentury urban development, and sought to ensure the same fight would not happen in the case of Grand Central Station. Through the creation of the Landmarks Preservation Commission (LPC), New York City sought to ensure that Grand Central would remain an historical landmark. *Penn Central,* however, sued, arguing that they had lost economic rights to future development revenues, including height in the high-density Midtown East district. Ultimately, the court ruled in favor of the LPC using the ad hoc multi-factor balancing test outlined above.

23 See, e.g., Harvey, 1987, *A Brief History of Neoliberalism.* See also: Brenner, 2004, *New State Spaces.*

24 Haag and Kolodner, 2023, "'The Untouchables.'

25 Ibid.

26 "Manhattanville—Final Environmental Impact Statement," 2007, New York City Department of City Planning (DCP).

27 "Manhattanville," 2007: S-21, 27.

28 "Manhattanville," 2007: S-10; 13.

29 "Manhattanville," 2007: S-85, 93.
30 Hernandez, 2022, "'Gym Crow.'"
31 "1968: Columbia In Crisis," 2024.
32 Ibid.
33 It is worth noting that the gym was envisioned to be used only by Columbia affiliates, and not the broader community, in the public park. For more on the 1968 demonstrations, see: "Student Demonstrators Take Over Hamilton Hall;" *Columbia Daily Spectator.*
34 De La Cruz, 1998, "Columbia University 1968."
35 Mann, 2018, "The Historic 1968 Struggle Against Columbia University."
36 Mann, 2018. The President of the Ford Foundation at the time, McGeorge Bundy, was a former White House National Security Affairs Advisor in the Johnson Administration and supporter of US involvement in the Vietnam War.
37 "Bitterness Rises Over Plans to Buy More Buildings in Morningside Heights," 1964, *The New York Times.*
38 Junker, 2020, "Preservation Through the Self-Help Housing Movement."
39 Huxtable, 1970, "Columbia Plan Includes Underground Expansion." *The New York Times.*
40 Lau, 2022, "Overgrown Ivy?" See also: Destin, 2024, "Between St. Nicholas and Amsterdam;" Pirani, 2022, "Fighting Gentrification."
41 UFAD New York Branch, 2022, "Columbia University Moves to Further Gentrify Harlem, Residents and Students Unite in Opposition," *The United Front Against Displacement,* https://theunitedfrontagainstdisplacement.org/urban-core/columbia-university-moves-to-further-gentrify-harlem-residents-and-students-unite-in-opposition/.
42 The following works by Baldwin are of particular interest: Baldwin, 2021, *In The Shadow of the Ivory Tower*; Baldwin, 2017, "When Universities Swallow Cities;" Baldwin, 2015, "The '800-Pound Gargoyle.'".

Chapter 1

1 O'Neill, 2021, "Planning Law." Spring 2021 syllabus, Columbia University Graduate School of Architecture, Planning, and Preservation (GSAPP), 1. Emphasis mine.
2 Steinhouse, 2024, "PLAN 6052: Planning Law." Spring 2024 syllabus, Columbia GSAPP, 1. Emphasis mine.
3 Rose, 2013, *Legal Foundations of Land Use Planning.*
4 Rose, 2013: 419. Emphasis mine.
5 Ibid., 419.
6 Jourdan and Strauss, 2016, *Planning for Wicked Problems.*
7 Ibid., 109.

8 Rose, 2013: 421.
9 Jourdan and Strauss, 2016: 109–10.
10 *Berman v. Parker*, 13.
11 Ibid., 33.
12 For more on LULUs and their relationship to land values, see: Opsal and Malin, 2020, "Prisons as LULUs." See also: Schively, 2007, "Understanding the NIMBY and LULU Phenomena."
13 Jourdan and Strauss, 2016: 131, 192.
14 The Municipal Art Society (MAS), today an advocacy and civil society organization in New York City focused on urbanism and public and aesthetic beauty, was founded in resistance to Penn Central's planned demolition (see: https://www.mas.org/about-us/history/).
15 See Pankin, 2020, "Our Guide to Highest and Best use in Real Estate," and "How To Determine The Highest and Best Use of a Property."
16 Spool, 2014, "Highest and Best Use Analysis."
17 Ibid.
18 See: Madden and Marcuse, 2016, *In Defense of Housing*, 25. See also: Smith, 1996, *The New Urban Frontier*, 62.
19 Engels, 1872 [republished 2021], *The Housing Question*. 23. See also: Harvey, 2008, "The Right to the City."
20 Newman and Wyly, 2006, "The Right to Stay Put, Revisited," 49.
21 Glaeser, 2013, "Ease Housing Regulation to Increase Supply." See also: Husock, 2013, "The Frozen City."
22 The court anticipated that the project could preserve or create six thousand jobs and enhance the city's tax base.
23 "Environmental Law Reporter Digest," 1981, "Poletown Neighborhood Council v. City of Detroit."
24 McGeehan, 2009, "Pfizer to Leave City That Won Land-Use Case." See also: Bullock, 2010, "The End of an Eminent Domain Error."
25 *Kelo v. City of New London.*
26 Ibid., 1.
27 Ibid., 8.
28 McGeehan, 2009, "Pfizer to Leave City."
29 Rose, 2013: 443.
30 Ibid.
31 Ibid., 444.
32 Ibid., 445.
33 *Denver Urban Renewal Authority v. Cook 186 Colo. 182, 526 P.2d 652 (1974).*
34 Heller, 2008, *The Gridlock Economy*. For a critical commentary alongside Heller's work, see also: Epstein, 2009, "Heller's Gridlock Economy in Perspective.

Chapter 2

1 "Manhattanville."

2 Ibid.

3 "Columbia University Manhattanville Campus Project Overview."

4 Commentary on the use of POPS in New York City is widespread in the urban planning literature, with critics raising questions about the extent to which POPS feel inclusive and inviting to all. Notably, these spaces typically come with zoning and land-use benefits, allowing for flexibility regarding building size, Floor-to-Area Ratio (FAR), or height. See: Kayden, 2000; Schmidt, Nemeth, and Botsford, 2011; Thomas, 2017; "New York City's POPS," 2022.

5 "Columbia University Manhattanville Campus Project Overview."

6 "Manhattanville," 2017.

7 Kilgore-Brown and Milligan, 2023, "Columbia Promised Manhattanville Campus Space to the Community. Accessing it is Another Story."

8 Cormier 2009, "Questioning M'Ville."

9 Kilgore-Brown and Milligan, 2023.

10 McKee, 2023, "Columbia's Tax Exemptions Exceed its Annual Community Investment by Millions." See more about these tax exemption's through the portal at NYC Open Data, titled "Property Exemption Details": https://data.cityofnewyork.us/City-Government/Property-Exemption-Detail/muvi-b6kx/data.

11 McKee, 2023.

12 Daar, 2007, "Eminent Domain: Properties, Principles, and Strange Bedfellows." *The Current: A Journal of Contemporary Politics, Culture, and Jewish Affairs at Columbia University,* http://www.columbia-current.org/eminent-domain.html.

13 Jones, David R. 2024. "Harlem Activists Aim to Tap The Brakes On Columbia Expansion." Community Service Society of New York. July 18. Accessed May 16, 2025. Available at: https://www.cssny.org/news/entry/harlem-activists-aim-to-tap-the-brakes-on-columbia-expansion.

14 Shoemaker, 2014, "Just Compensation," *The Columbia Political Review,* https://www.cpreview.org/articles/2014/11/just-compensation.

15 Williams, 2008, "2 Gas Stations, and a Family's Resolve, Confront Columbia Expansion Plan."

16 Amzallag, 2008, "Court Dismisses Lawsuit Against CU.".

17 "Chapter 28: Response to Comments."

18 For more information about WE ACT, see: http://weact.nyc/tabid/180/Default.aspx.

19 "Chapter 28: Response to Comments."
20 Ibid.
21 Ibid.
22 "Community Board 9: 197-A Plan," 2008, A 197-a plan as adopted by the City Planning Commission and the City Council, DCP #08-03, https://www.nyc.gov/assets/planning/download/pdf/community/197a-plans/mn9_hamilton_manhattanville_197a.pdf.
23 "CB9 197-a Plan," 2024, *The City of New York, Manhattan Community Board 9,* https://www.cb9m.org/197a_plan.
24 "The Time Has Come," 2005, *WE ACT for Environmental Justice (West Harlem Environmental Action).*
25 Ibid., 6.
26 "Community Board 9 Manhattan 197-a Plan Brief," 2007, *New York City Planning Commission.*
27 Ibid., 4.
28 Ibid., 5.
29 Ibid., 21.
30 "Appendix N: CB9 197-A Plan Alternative Plan 1: Impact Analyses," 2007.
31 Ibid., N.1-26, N.1-27, N.1-28, N.1-24, N.2-1-3, respectively.
32 Shoemaker, 2014.
33 Dorsey, 2016, "Making Community Benefits Agreements Count," *Shelterforce.*
34 Ibid. See also: "Community Commitments," 2024, *Columbia Neighbors, The Office of Public Affairs and The Office of Government & Community Affairs..*
35 "West Harlem Community Benefits Agreement," 2009, *West Harlem Development Corporation.*
36 Dorsey, 2016.
37 "West Harlem Community Benefits Agreement," 2009, 2.
38 Ibid., 10–13.
39 Ibid., 16.
40 Ibid., 18.
41 Paul, 2009, "Columbia University's Expansion and the Struggle for the Future of Harlem," *Planners Network.*
42 Learn more about Maxine Griffith in "Maxine Griffith."
43 Ibid.
44 Pacheco, 2020, "Black Columbia GSAPP Faculty and Students Push School for Comprehensive Reforms."
45 Ibid.

46 See the following illustrative articles: "UFAD Activists Work Alongside Manhattanville Tenants Facing Poor Living Conditions," 2023, "After Displacement from Manhattanville, a Community Remains Resilient." *Columbia Spectator*; Hardy and Santos-Espino, 2023, "Manhattanville Tenants and the United Front Against Displacement Call for Better Living Conditions in NYCHA Housing;" and Carlson and Zapana, 2008, "In A New York Minute."

Chapter 3

1 "Manhattanville," 2017.
2 "Columbia University Manhattanville Campus Project Overview."
1 See O'Neill, 2021; Steinhouse, 2024.
2 *Penn Central vs. New York City* (1978).
3 See *First English Evangelical Lutheran Church v. Los Angeles County* (1987).
4 See *Tahoe-Sierra Preservation Council, Inc. v. Tahoe Regional Planning Agency* (2002).
5 See Heller, 2008; Epstein, 2000.
6 Caro, 1974.
7 While this is true of many of Moses's parkways, it is not true of the Cross Bronx Expressway, which is built for cars, busses, trucks, and other vehicles (Caro, 1974).
8 "West Harlem Community Benefits Agreement," 2009.
9 *Berman v. Parker* (1954).

Chapter 4

1 For more on Denver's history of displacement in Auraria, see Summers (2003), Bryson (2018). For more on District Six and the CPUT campus in Cape Town, see Charles (2020), Bantom (2024).
2 Sullivan, 2021, "Your Guide to Morningside Heights in Upper Manhattan."
3 Junker, 2020.
4 Baldwin, 2021, *In the Shadow of the Ivory Tower.* See also: Baldwin, 2017; Baldwin, 2015.
5 Baldwin, 2015: 93.
6 "Displaced Aurarians Neighborhood Memory Project."
7 Perez-Kindle, 2023, "Oral History of Sheila Pere."
8 Ibid.

9 Gomez and Gomez-Delgado, 2022, "Oral History of Greg and Rita Gomez-Delgado."

10 More about the District Six Museum available here: https://www.districtsix.co.za/.

11 Coombes, 2003, "District Six: The Archaeology of Memory," 116–18. See also McEachern, 1998, "Working with Memory," 48–72.

12 McEachern, 1998: 48.

13 Sociologist Doug McAdam coined the term "oppositional consciousness" when exploring youth organizing movements in the context of twentieth-century Black political organizing. See McAdam and Tarrow, 2018, "The Political Context of Social Movements," 19–42.

14 Healey, 1997, *Collaborative Planning.*

15 Davidoff, 1965, "Advocacy and Pluralism in Planning."

16 *Kelo v. City of New London* (2005).

17 I engage seminal works by John Dewey, including the following: Dewey, 1986, "The Future of Radical Political Action;" Dewey, 1987a, "The Future of Liberalism;" and Dewey, 1987b, "Democracy Is Radical."

18 "West Harlem Community Benefits Agreement." 2009.

19 Smith, 2006, *Uses of Heritage.*

20 Smith, 2012, "Discourses of Heritage : Implications for Archaeological Community Practice," *Nuevo Mundo.*

21 Ignaccolo, et al., 2023, "Exclusionary Tales in Beirut's Spaces of Craftsmanship," *Abstracts of the International Cartographic Association.*

22 For more on Ignaccolo and colleagues' innovative digital mapping exercise in Beirut, see: https://themetropole.blog/2024/07/24/digital-summer-school-living-heritage-atlas-beirut-mapping-and-activating-beiruts-crafts/

23 Fullilove and Wallace, 2011, "Serial Forced Displacement in American Cities,," 381.

24 Sclar, N.D., "House Housing: An Untimely History of Architecture and Real Estate." See also: Schwartz, 1993, *The New York Approach.*

25 Wilkerson, 2011, *The Warmth of Other Suns."*

26 Wilson, 2020, "Opinion: Urbanism is Complicit in Infra-Structural Racism."

27 Baffoe, 2023, "Neoliberal Urban Development and the Polarization of Urban Governance." See also Troiani and Dutson, 2021, "The Neoliberal University as a Space to Learn/Think/Work in Higher Education," 5; Morley, 2023, "The Systemic Neoliberal Colonisation of Higher Education," 1–16.

28 Morley, 2023: 9. See also: Giroux, 2014, *Neoliberalism's War on Higher Education.*

REFERENCES

Primary Cases

Berman v. Parker 348 U. S. 26, (1954).

Denver Urban Renewal Authority v. Cook, 186 Colo. 182, 526 P.2d 652 (1974).

First English Evangelical Lutheran Church v. Los Angeles County, 482 U.S. 304 (1987).

Kelo v. City of New London, 545 U.S. 469 (2005).

Lucas v South Carolina, 505 US 1003 (1992).

Masheter v. Oido Holding Co., 38 Ohio App.2d 49, 313 N.E.2d 413 (1973)

Penn Central vs. New York City, 438 U.S. 104 (1978).

Pierson v. Post, 3 Cai. R. 175 (1805), New York Court of Appeals.

Poletown Council v. Detroit, 410 Mich. 616 (1981).

State of Louisiana, Dept. of Highways v. Crow, 286 So.2d 353 (Louisiana, 1973).

Tahoe-Sierra Preservation Council, Inc. v. Tahoe Regional Planning Agency, 535 U.S. 302 (2002).

Primary Syllabi

O'Neill, Moira. 2021. "Planning Law." Spring 2021 syllabus. Columbia University Graduate School of Architecture, Planning, and Preservation (GSAPP).

Steinhouse, Kurt. 2024. "PLAN 6052: Planning Law." Spring 2024 syllabus. Columbia University Graduate School of Architecture, Planning, and Preservation (GSAPP).

Secondary Sources

"1968: Columbia In Crisis." 2024. *Columbia University Libraries: 1968 Retrospective*

Exhibition. Accessed 13 June 2024. Available at: https://exhibitions.library.columbia.edu/exhibits/show/1968/protests.

"2023 Manhattanville in West Harlem Implementation Plan Report." 2024. *Columbia Neighbors.* The Office of Public Affairs and The Office of Government & Community Affairs. Accessed 11 July 2024. Available at: https://neighbors.columbia.edu/content/2023-manhattanville-west-harlem-implementation-plan-report.

"A Vision for Long-Range Planning." 2024. *The Governor's Office of Planning and Research (OPR).* Accessed 31 May 2024. Available at: https://opr.ca.gov/docs/OPR_C2_final.pdf.

Amzallag, Daniel. 2008. "Court Dismisses Lawsuit Against CU." *The Columbia Spectator.* September 26. Accessed 11 July 2024. Available at: https://www.columbiaspectator.com/2008/09/26/court-dismisses-lawsuit-against-cu/.

"Appendix N: CB9 197-A Plan Alternative Plan 1: Impact Analyses." 2007. *New York City Department of City Planning (DCP).* Accessed 1 May 2024. Available at: https://www.nyc.gov/assets/planning/download/pdf/applicants/env-review/manhattanville/app_n.pdf.

Appleton, Barry. 2002. "Regulatory Takings: The International Law Perspective." *NYU Environmental Law Journal.* Vol. 11. Held at the New York Law School Digital Commons. Available at: https://digitalcommons.nyls.edu/cgi/viewcontent.cgi?article=2485&context=-fac_articles_chapters.

Baffoe, Gideon. 2023. "Neoliberal Urban Development and the Polarization of Urban Governance." *Cities.* 143: 104570. 1–5. Available at: https://doi.org/10.1016/j.cities.2023.104570.

Bagli, Charles. 2010. "Court Upholds Columbia Campus Expansion Plan." *The New York Times.* 25 June. Accessed 9 November 2023. https://www.nytimes.com/2010/06/25/nyregion/25columbia.html.

Baldwin, Davarian L. 2021. *In The Shadow of the Ivory Tower: How Universities Are Plundering Our Cities.* New York: Bold Type Books.

Baldwin, Davarian L. 2017. "When Universities Swallow Cities." *The Chronicle of Higher Education.* 30. 1–7. 30 July. Accessed 26 February 2025. Available at: https://www.chronicle.com/article/when-universities-swallow-cities/.

Baldwin, Davarian L. 2015. "The '800-Pound Gargoyle': The Long History of Higher Education and Urban Development on Chicago's South Side." *American Quarterly*. 67(1): 81–103.

Bantom, Kaylynne. 2024. "'We Won't Forget': District Six Residents Remember Fateful Day of Forced Removals." *News24.* February 13. Accessed 15 July 2024. Available at: https://www.news24.com/news24/community-newspaper/peoples-post/we-wont-forget-district-six-residents-remember-fateful-day-of-forced-removals-20240213.

Bethany R. Berger. 2006. "It's Not About the Fox: The Untold History of Pierson v. Post." 55. *Duke Law Journal* 1089-1143. Available at: https://scholarship.law.duke.edu/dlj/vol55/iss6/.

Berman, Marshall, 1981. *All That Is Solid Melts into Air: The Experience of Modernity*. New York: Simon and Schuster.

"Bitterness Rises Over Plans to Buy More Buildings in Morningside Heights." 1964. *The New York Times.* January 18. Accessed March 30. Available at: https://www.nytimes.com/1964/01/18/archives/morningside-heights-is-having-growing-pains-and-strain-shows-on.html.

Brenner, Neil. 2004. *New State Spaces: Urban Governance and the Rescaling of Statehood.* Oxford, Oxfordshire, U.K.: Oxford University Press.

Briffault, Richard. 2000. "Localism and Regionalism." *Buffalo Law Review.* 48 Buff. L. Rev. 1. Available at: https://scholarship.law.columbia.edu/faculty_scholarship/925.

Bryson, Donna. 2018. "In the '60s, Denver Decided to Replace this Community with the Auraria Campus. Here's What it Lost." *Denverite.* November 5. Accessed July 1 2024. Available at: https://denverite.com/2018/11/05/denver-auraria-history-displacement/.

Bullock, Scott. 2010. "The End of an Eminent Domain Error: Pfizer Closes in New London." *The Institute for Justice.* February 2. Accessed July 3, 2024. Available at: https://ij.org/ll/the-end-of-an-eminent-domain-error-pfizer-closes-in-new-london/.

Carlson, Raymond and Victor Zapana. 2008. "In A New York Minute, Aid Vs. Displacement." *Yale Daily News.* January 25. Accessed 13 April 2024. Available at: https://yaledailynews.com/blog/2008/01/25/in-a-new-york-minute-aid-vs-displacement/.

Caro, Robert A. 1974. *The Power Broker : Robert Moses and the Fall of New York.* New York: Knopf.

"CB9 197-a Plan." 2024. The City of New York, Manhattan Community Board 9. Accessed 11 July 2024. Available at: https://www.cb9m.org/197a_plan.

"Chapter 28: Response to Comments." N.D. New York City Department of City Planning (NYC DCP) Draft Environmental Impact Statement (DEIS). Accessed 10 July 2024. Available at: https://www.nyc.gov/assets/planning/download/pdf/applicants/env-review/manhattanville/28.pdf/

Charles, Marvin. 2020. "Fragments of Demolished District Six Homes to be Placed on Memorial Wall." *IOL News.* July 21. Accessed 17 July 2024. Available at: https://www.iol.co.za/news/south-africa/western-cape/fragments-of-demolished-district-six-homes-to-be-placed-on-memorial-wall-51239705.

"Community Board 9: 197-A Plan." 2008. A 197-a plan as adopted by the City Planning Commission and the City Council. DCP #08-03. Accessed 11 July 2024. Available at: https://www.nyc.gov/assets/planning/download/pdf/community/197a-plans/mn9_hamilton_manhattanville_197a.pdf.

"Community Board 9 Manhattan 197-a Plan Brief." 2007. New York City Planning Commission. Document #N 060047 NPM. Accessed 1 July 2024. 1–42. Available at: https://www.cb9m.org/pdf-archives/transcripts-project-plans/197a-plan-brief.pdf.

"Community Commitments." 2024. *Columbia Neighbors.* The Office of Public Affairs and The Office of Government & Community Affairs. Accessed 11 July 2024. Available at: https://neighbors.columbia.edu/content/community-commitments.

"Community Benefits Agreement." 2024. *Columbia Office of Public Affairs.* Accessed 11 July 2024. Available at: https://neighbors.columbia.edu/content/community-commitments. https://communications.news.columbia.edu/content/community-benefits-agreement.

"Columbia University Manhattanville Campus Project Overview." N.D. *Columbia University Manhattanville Campus Masterplan.* Accessed 10 July 2024. Available at: https://neighbors.columbia.edu/sites/default/files/content/Manhattanville%20Campus%20Project%20Overview.pdf.

Coombes, Annie E. 2003. "District Six: The Archaeology of Memory." *History after Apartheid: Visual Culture and Public Memory in a Democratic South Africa.* 116–148. Durham, NC: Duke University Press.

Cormier, Amanda. 2009. "Questioning M'Ville." *The Columbia Spectator.* 10 December. Accessed 8 July 2024. https://spectatorarchive.library.columbia.edu/?a=d&d=cs20091210-02.2.3&srpos=1&e=-------en-20--1--txt-txIN-%e2%80%9cQuestioning+M%e2%80%99Ville%2c%e2%80%9d+------.

Daar, Evan. 2007. "Eminent Domain: Properties, Principles, and Strange Bedfellows." *The Current: A Journal of Contemporary Politics, Culture, and Jewish Affairs at Columbia University.* Winter 2007. Accessed 1 July 2024. Available at: http://www.columbia-current.org/eminent-domain.html.

Davidoff, Paul. 1965. "Advocacy and Pluralism in Planning." *Journal of the American Institute of Planners.* 31: 277–296.

De La Cruz, Frank. 1998. "Columbia University 1968: Personal Recollections." Accessed 13 June 2024. Available at: https://www.columbia.edu/cu/computinghistory/1968/.

Destin, Kathryn. 2024. "Between St. Nicholas and Amsterdam: How Columbia Claims 'Public Use' for its Private Gain." *Columbia Spectator.* February 19. Acessed 13 June 2024. Available at: https://www.columbiaspectator.com/opinion/2024/02/19/between-st-nicholas-and-amsterdam-how-columbia-claims-public-use-for-its-private-gain/.

Dewey, John. 1986. "The Future of Radical Political Action." In *The Later Works, 1925–1953, Vol. 9*, edited by Jo Ann Boydston, 66–70. Carbondale: Southern Illinois University Press.

Dewey, John. 1987a. "The Future of Liberalism." In *The Later Works, 1925–1953, Vol. 11*, edited by Jo Ann Boydston, 289–95. Carbondale: Southern Illinois University Press.

Dewey, John. 1987b. "Democracy Is Radical." In *The Later Works, 1925-1953, Vol. 11*, edited by Jo Ann Boydston, 296–99. Carbondale: Southern Illinois University Press.

"Displaced Aurarians Neighborhood Memory Project." N.D. *History-Colorado.* Accessed 5 January 2024. Available at: https://www.historycolorado.org/displaced-aurarians-neighborhood-memory-project#:~:text=The%20Displaced%20Aurarians%20Memory%20Project,shared%20Auraria%20Higher%20Education%20Campus.

Dorries, Heather. 2022. "What is Planning without Property? Relational Practices of Being and Belonging." *Environment and Planning D: Society and Space*, 40(2), 306-318. https://doi.org/10.1177/02637758211068505.

Dorsey, Sherrel. 2016. "Making Community Benefits Agreements Count." *Shelterforce.* October 21. Accessed 11 July 2024. Available at: https://shelterforce.org/2016/10/21/making-community-benefits-agreements-count/.

Ellickson, Robert C., Vicki L. Been, Roderick M. Hills, and Christopher Serkin. 2020. *Land Use Controls: Cases and Materials, 5th edition.* Aspen Casebook Series, Wolters Kluwer.

Engels, Friedrich. 1872 [republished in 2021]. *The Housing Question.* New York: International Publishing Company, Inc.

"Environmental Law Reporter Digest." 1981. "Poletown Neighborhood Council v. City of Detroit." *ELR: The Environmental Law Reporter. No. 66294 (304 N.W.2d 455, 410 Mich. 616, 19 ERC 1972) (Mich. March 13, 1981).* 11 ELR 20778. Accessed June 15 2024. Available at: https://www.elr.info/sites/default/files/litigation/11.20778.htm.

Epstein, Richard A. 2009. "Heller's Gridlock Economy in Perspective: Why There Is Too Little, Not Too Much, Private Property." John M. Olin Program in Law and Economics Working Paper. No. 495. Available through Chicago Unbound at: https://chicagounbound.uchicago.edu/cgi/viewcontent.cgi?article=1230&context=law_and_economics.

Forsyth, Ann. 2025. "Daring to Stop: Challenging Program-Level Learning Outcome Measurement in Urban Planning Accreditation." *Journal of Planning Education and Research.* OnlineFirst. Available at: https://doi.org/10.1177/0739456X251314198.

Forsyth, Ann. 2024. "Harvard University: Currently Accredited." *Plan-*

ning Accreditation Board (PAB). Accessed 31 May 2024. Available at: https://www.planningaccreditationboard.org/harvard-university/.

Frug, Gerald, Richard Ford, and David Barron. 2014. *Local Government Law, Cases and Materials, 6th (American Casebook Series) 6th Edition.* New York: West Academic Publishing.

Frug, Gerald E. 2001. *City Making: Building Communities without Building Walls.* Princeton, NJ: Princeton University Press.

Fullilove, Mindy Thompson, and Rodrick Wallace. 2011. "Serial Forced Displacement in American Cities, 1916–2010." *The Journal of Urban Health.* 88(3): 381–389. Doi: 10.1007/s11524-011-9585-2.

Giroux Henry A. 2014. *Neoliberalism's War on Higher Education.* London, U.K.: Haymarket Books.

Glaeser, Edward. 2013. "Ease Housing Regulation to Increase Supply." *The New York Times.* October 16. Accessed 4 July 2024. Available at: https://www.nytimes.com/roomfordebate/2013/10/16/housing-thats-not-a-luxury/ease-housing-regulation-to-increase-supply.

Gomez-Delgado, Greg, and Rita Gomez-Delgado. 2022. "Oral History of Greg and Rita

Gomez-Delgado." *I am Auraria Oral History Project.* HistoryColorado. December 31. Accessed July 17 2024. Available at: https://www.historycolorado.org/displaced-aurarians-neighborhood-memory-project#:~:text=The%20Displaced%20Aurarians%20Memory%20Project,shared%20Auraria%20Higher%20Education%20Campus.

Haag, Matthew, and Meredith Kolodner. 2023. "'The Untouchables': How Columbia and N.Y.U. Benefit From Huge Tax Breaks." *The New York Times.* September 26. Accessed 13 June 2024. Available at: https://www.nytimes.com/2023/09/26/nyregion/columbia-university-property-tax-nyc.html.

Hardy, Elena and Sharon Santos-Espino. 2023. "Manhattanville Tenants and the United Front Against Displacement Call for Better Living Conditions in NYCHA Housing." *The Columbia Daily Spectator.* March 29. Accessed 11 July 2024. Available at: https://www.columbiaspectator.com/city-news/2023/03/29/manhattanville-tenants-and-the-united-front-against-displacement-call-for-better-living-conditions-in-nycha-housing/.

Harvey, David. 2008. "The Right to the City." *New Left Review.* Vol.

53, no. ii, Sept/Oct. Available online at: https://newleftreview.org/issues/ii53/articles/david-harvey-the-right-to-the-city.

Harvey, David. 1987. *A Brief History of Neoliberalism.* Oxford, Oxfordshire, U.K.: Oxford University Press.

Healey, Patsy. 1997. *Collaborative Planning: Shaping Places in Fragmented Societies*. London, England: Macmillan Press Ltd.

Heller, Michael. 2008. *The Gridlock Economy: How Too Much Ownership Wrecks Markets, Stops Innovation, and Costs Lives.* New York: Basic Books.

Hernandez, Jorge. 2022. "'Gym Crow': Looking Back on the 1968 Morningside Gym Protests." *The Columbia Spectator.* February 15. Accessed 15 May 2024. Available at: https://www.columbiaspectator.com/sports/2022/02/15/gym-crow-looking-back-on-the-1968-morningside-gym-protests/.

Husock, Howard. 2013. "The Frozen City." *City Journal: Special Issue: The Social Order, States and Cities, Economy, Finance, and Budgets.* Available online at: https://www.city-journal.org/article/the-frozen-city.

Huxtable, Ada Louise. 1970. "Columbia Plan Includes Underground Expansion." *The New York Times.* February 18. Accessed June 13 2024. Available at: https://www.nytimes.com/1970/02/18/archives/columbia-plan-includes-underground-expansion-columbia-master-plan.html.

Ignaccolo, Carmelo, et al. 2023. "Exclusionary Tales in Beirut's Spaces of Craftsmanship." *Abstracts of the International Cartographic Association, 6, 97, 2023.* 31st International Cartographic Conference (ICC 2023), 13–18 August 2023, Cape Town, South Africa. https://doi.org/10.5194/ica-abs-6-97-2023.

Jourdan, Dawn, and Eric J. Strauss. 2016. *Planning for Wicked Problems: A Planner's Guide to Land Use Law.* New York: Routledge.

Junker, Emily. 2020. "Preservation Through The Self-Help Housing Movement." Submitted in partial fulfillment for the degree of Master of Science in Urban Planning (MSUP) and Historic Preservation (HP) at Columbia University's Graduate School of Architecture, Planning, and Preservation (GSAPP), New York, New York. Available at: https://doi.org/10.7916/d8-e539-6r88.

Kayden, Jerold. 2000. *Privately Owned Public Space: The New York City Experience.* New York: Wiley. Written with contributions from the

New York City Department of City Planning (NYC DCP) and the Municipal Art Society of New York (MAS).

"Kelo v. New London." N.d. *Oyez*, www.oyez.org/cases/2004/04-108. Accessed 3 Jul. 2024.

Kensinger, Nathan. 2018. "As Columbia University Moves into Manhattanville, its Industrial Past is Erased." *Curbed NY.* 8 March. Accessed 9 November 2023. https://ny.curbed.com/2018/3/8/17095838/manhattanville-columbia-university-expansion-photo-essay.

Kilgore-Brown, Lilienne, and Eden Milligan. 2023. "Columbia Promised Manhattanville Campus Space to the Community. Accessing it is Another Story." *Columbia Spectator. XXXIII(2).* November 3. Accessed 5 July 2024. Available at: https://www.columbiaspectator.com/the-eye/2023/11/03/columbia-promised-manhattanville-campus-space-to-the-community-accessing-it-is-another-story/.

Krueckeberg, Donald A. 1995. "The Difficult Character of Property: To Whom Do Things Belong?" *Journal of the American Planning Association.* 61(3), 301–309. https://doi-org.ezproxy.cul.columbia.edu/10.1080/01944369508975644.

Madden, David, and Peter Marcuse. 2016. *In Defense of Housing: The Politics of Crisis.* New York: Verso.

"Manhattanville: Reflections on a 21st-Century Campus Columbia's bold vision for a new city campus begins to take shape." 2017. *Columbia Magazine.* Spring. Accessed 9 July 2024. Available at: https://magazine.columbia.edu/article/manhattanville-reflections-21st-century-campus.

"Manhattanville—Final Environmental Impact Statement." 2007. *New York City Department of City Planning (DCP).* November 16. Accessed 1 June 2024. Available at: https://www.nyc.gov/site/planning/applicants/env-review/manhattanville-west-harlem.page.

Mann, Eric. 2018. "The Historic 1968 Struggle Against Columbia University." *Verso Books: Blog Post.* 7 May. Accessed 8 June 2024. Available at: https://www.versobooks.com/blogs/news/3790-the-historic-1968-struggle-against-columbia-university.

Marsh, Mary. 2018. "After Displacement from Manhattanville, a Community Remains Resilient." *Columbia Spectator: The Eye Logform Features.* XXV(7). November 16. Accessed 1 June 2024. Available at: https://www.columbiaspectator.com/the-eye/2018/11/16/what-happened-to-the-residents-of-602-west-132nd-st/.

"Maxine Griffith." N.D. *Columbia University Graduate School of Architecture, Planning, and Preservation (GSAPP).* Accessed 11 July 2024. Available at: https://www.arch.columbia.edu/faculty/607-maxine-griffith.

McAdam, Doug and Sidney Tarrow. 2018. "The Political Context of Social Movements." In: *The Wiley Blackwell Companion to Social Movements: Facilitative and Constraining Contexts and Conditions.* David Snow, Sarah Soule, Hanspeter Kriesi, and Holly McCammon, eds. 19–42. Hoboken, New Jersey: John Wiley and Sons.

McEachern, Charmaine. 1998. "Working with Memory: The District Six Museum in the New South Africa." *Social Analysis: The International Journal of Social and Cultural Practice.* 42(2): 48–72. http://www.jstor.org/stable/23166569.

McGeehan, Patrick. 2009. "Pfizer to Leave City That Won Land-Use Case." *The New York Times.* November 13. Accessed 2 July 2024. Available at: https://www.nytimes.com/2009/11/13/nyregion/13pfizer.html.

McKee, Amira. 2023. "Columbia's Tax Exemptions Exceed its Annual Community Investment by Millions. West Harlem Residents Want More." *Columbia Spectator.* Graphic by Jenny Ye, Illustration by Katya Reichert. October 27. Accessed 10 July 2024. Available at: https://www.columbiaspectator.com/city-news/2023/10/27/columbias-tax-exemptions-exceed-its-annual-community-investment-by-millions-west-harlem-residents-want-more/.

Morley Christine. 2023. "The Systemic Neoliberal Colonisation of Higher Education: A Critical Analysis of the Obliteration of Academic Practice." *Australian Education Research.* 1–16. March 1. Accessed 19 July 2024. Doi: 10.1007/s13384-023-00613-z.

"New York City's Privately Owned Public Spaces (POPS)." 2022. *New York City Department of City Planning (DCP).* Accessed 10 July 2024. Available at: https://www.nyc.gov/site/planning/plans/pops/pops.page.

Newman, Kathe and Elvin K. Wyly. 2006. "The Right to Stay Put, Revisited: Gentrification and Resistance to Displacement in New York City." *Urban Studies.* 43(1): 23–57.

Opsal, Tara, and Stephanie A. Malin. 2020. "Prisons as LULUs: Understanding the Parallels between Prison Proliferation and Environmental Injustices." *Sociological Inquiry.* 90(3): 579–602.

"PAB Accreditation Standards and Criteria." 2021. *Planning Accreditation Board.* January. Accessed May 31 2024. Available at: https://www.planningaccreditationboard.org/wp-content/uploads/2021/01/2017Standards.pdf.

Pacheco, Antonio. 2020. "Black Columbia GSAPP Faculty and Students Push School for Comprehensive Reforms." *Archinet.* June 30. Accessed 5 June 2024. Available at: https://archinect.com/news/article/150204915/black-columbia-gsapp-faculty-and-students-push-school-for-comprehensive-reforms.

Pankin, Joshua. 2020. "Our Guide to Highest and Best use in Real Estate." *Altus Group.* November 13. Accessed 3 June 2024. Available at: https://www.altusgroup.com/insights/highest-and-best-use-real-estate-appraisal/?utm_source=google&utm_medium=organic.

Paul, Brian. 2009. "Columbia University's Expansion and the Struggle for the Future of Harlem." *Planners Network.* October. Accessed 11 July 2024. Available at: https://www.plannersnetwork.org/2009/10/columbia-universitys-expansion-and-the-struggle-for-the-future-of-harlem/.

Perez-Kindle, Sheila. 2023. "Oral History of Sheila Perez." *I am Auraria Oral History Project.* HistoryColorado. April 11. Accessed July 17 2024. Available at: https://www.historycolorado.org/displaced-aurarians-neighborhood-memory-project#:~:text=The%20Displaced%20Aurarians%20Memory%20Project,shared%20Auraria%20Higher%20Education%20Campus.

Pirani, Alykhan. 2022. "Fighting Gentrification: Litigation is Not "the Only Source of Support."" *Columbia Undergraduate Law Review.* February 15. Accessed 13 June 2022. Available at: https://www.culawreview.org/journal/fighting-gentrification-litigation-is-not-the-only-source-of-support#:~:text=Many%20Harlem%20residents%20fear%20that,for%20generations%20and%20depend%20on.

PropertyMetrics.com. 2023. "How To Determine The Highest and Best Use of a Property." *PropertyMetrics.com.* January 2. Accessed 3 July 2024. Available at: https://propertymetrics.com/blog/highest-and-best-use/.

Povinelli, Elizabeth. 2016. *Geontologies: A Requiem to Late Liberalism.* Durham, NC: Duke University Press.

Rose, Carol M. 1985. "Possession as the Origin of Property." Faculty Scholarship Series. Paper 1830. Yale Digital Commons. http://digitalcommons.law.yale.edu/fss_papers/1830.

Rose, Jerome G. 2013. *Legal Foundations of Land Use Planning: Textbook-Casebook and Materials on Planning Law 1st Edition.* New York: Routledge.

Rusk, David. 2010. *Cities without Suburbs: A Census 2010 Perspective.* Baltimore: Johns Hopkins University Press.

Saghir, Chade and Gary Sand. 2015. "What Do City Planners Need to Know? When Do They Need to Know It?" *International Journal of Social Science Studies.* 3(2): 21–29.

Schwartz, Joel. 1993. *The New York Approach: Robert Moses, Urban Liberals, and Redevelopment of the Inner City.* Columbus, OH: Ohio State University Press.

Sclar, Elliott. N.D. "House Housing: An Untimely History of Architecture and Real Estate." Columbia University Temple Hoyne Buell Center for the Study of American Architecture. Accessed 19 July 2024. Available at: https://househousing.buellcenter.columbia.edu/#House-Housing-Economies-of-One-Type-or-Another.

Smith, Laurajane. 2006. *Uses of Heritage.* London and New York: Routledge.

———. 2012. "Discourses of Heritage : Implications for Archaeological Community Practice," *Nuevo Mundo* [Online]. 5 October 2012. Accessed July 7, 2025. https://doi.org/10.4000/nuevomundo.64148.

Spool, Philip G. 2014. "Highest and Best Use Analysis." *Working RE.* Accessed 1 July 2024. Available at: https://www.workingre.com/highest-best-use-analysis-2/. "Student Demonstrators Take Over Hamilton Hall; Administration Refuses to Talk 'Under Coercion'; 1 Arrested in Park In Violent Protest." 1968. *Columbia Daily Spectator.* Volume CXII, Number 101, 24 April 1968. Accessed 1 June 2024. Available at: https://spectatorarchive.library.columbia.edu/?a=d&d=cs19680424-01.2.2&e=-------en-20--1--txt-tx-IN-------.

Sullivan, Deidre. 2021. "Your Guide to Morningside Heights in Upper Manhattan." *StreetEasy.* July 21. Accessed 17 July 2024. Available at:

https://streeteasy.com/blog/morningside-heights-manhattan-neighborhood/.

Summers, Jodi. 2003. "Auraria: From Neighborhood to Campus." *Auraria Library.* Submitted in partial fulfillment for the degree of Master of Arts in History and Urban and Regional Planning at the University of Colorado (CU) Denver, Denver, CO. Available at: https://digital.auraria.edu/work/ns/5a646167-2003-4de5-9486-7dc3f1783d06.

Lau, Tandy. 2022. "Overgrown Ivy?: Columbia University's Encroachment on Harlem Sparks Campus Protest." *New York Amsterdam News.* September 29. Accessed 13 June 2024. Available at: https://amsterdamnews.com/news/2022/09/29/overgrown-ivy-columbia-universitys-encroachment-on-harlem-sparks-campus-protest/.

Schively, C. 2007. "Understanding the NIMBY and LULU Phenomena: Reassessing Our Knowledge Base and Informing Future Research." *Journal of Planning Literature.* 21(3): 255-266.

Schmidt, Stephan, Jeremy Nemeth, and Erik Botsford. 2011. "The Evolution of Privately Owned Public Spaces in New York City." *Urban Design International.* 16(4): 270–284.

Shoemaker, SM. 2014. "Just Compensation." *The Columbia Political Review.* November. Accessed 20 June 2024. Available at: https://www.cpreview.org/articles/2014/11/just-compensation.

Smith, Neil. 1996. *The New Urban Frontier: Gentrification and the Revanchist City.* New York: Routledge.

Song, Lily. 2021. "Reparative Planning as Movement Building." *Planetizen.* August 25. Accessed 19 July 2024. Available at: https://www.planetizen.com/features/114461-reparative-planning-movement-building.

"The HBS Case Method." 2014. *Harvard Business School.* Accessed 31 May 2024. Available at: https://www.hbs.edu/mba/academic-experience/Pages/the-hbs-case-method.aspx.

"The Time Has Come." 2005. WE ACT for Environmental Justice (West Harlem Environmental Action). Accessed 11 July 2024. Available at: http://weact.nyc/Portals/7/FINAL%20CASE%20STATEMENT.pdf.

Thomas, Kelsey. 2017. "NYC Official: Time to Review City's Not-So-Public Public Spaces." *Next City.* April 21. Accessed 1 July 2024.

Available at: https://nextcity.org/urbanist-news/nyc-privately-owned-public-spaces-access-audit-POPS-report.

"Title 7. Planning And Land Use." 2024. California Government Code - Gov [65000 – 66499.58]. The State Legislature of California. Accessed 31 May 2024. Available at: https://leginfo.legislature.ca.gov/faces/codes_displaySection.xhtml?sectionNum=65302.&lawCode=GOV.

Troiani, Igea, and Claudia Dutson. 2021. "The Neoliberal University as a Space to Learn/Think/Work in Higher Education." *Architecture and Culture*. 9(1): 5–23. doi:10.1080/20507828.2021.1898836.

Tuckness, Alex. 2020. "Locke's Political Philosophy." *Stanford Encyclopedia of Philosophy.* First published Wed Nov 9, 2005; substantive revision Tue Oct 6, 2020. Accessed 7 June 2024. Available at: https://plato.stanford.edu/entries/locke-political/.

"UFAD Activists Work Alongside Manhattanville Tenants Facing Poor Living Conditions." 2023. *Columbia Daily Spectator.* March 28. Accessed 18 April 2024. Available at: https://www.youtube.com/watch?v=KpBiHRdc0AM.

UFAD New York Branch. 2022. "Columbia University Moves to Further Gentrify Harlem, Residents and Students Unite in Opposition." *The United Front Against Displacement.* Accessed 13 June 2024. Available at: https://theunitedfrontagainstdisplacement.org/urban-core/columbia-university-moves-to-further-gentrify-harlem-residents-and-students-unite-in-opposition/.

Venkat, Surina. 2024. "Harlem Politicians, Community Advocates Announce Support for Bill to Halt Columbia's Expansion Projects at 'Juneteenth Rally for Housing Justice.'" *Columbia Spectator.* June 26. Accessed 8 July 2024. Available at: https://www.columbiaspectator.com/city-news/2024/06/26/harlem-politicians-community-advocates-announce-support-for-bill-to-halt-columbias-expansion-projects-at-juneteenth-rally-for-housing-justice/.

"West Harlem Community Benefits Agreement." 2009. *West Harlem Development Corporation.* Accessed 11 July 2024. Available at: https://westharlemdc.org/wp-content/uploads/2023/02/Community-Benefits-Agreement-May-18-2009.pdf

Wilkerson, Isabel. 2011. *The Warmth of Other Suns: The Epic Story of America's Great Migration*. New York: Vintage Books.

Williams, Timothy. 2008. "2 Gas Stations, and a Family's Resolve, Confront Columbia Expansion Plan." *The New York Times.* September 21. Accessed 3 July 2024. Available at: https://www.nytimes.com/2008/09/21/nyregion/21gas.html.

Wilson, Kea. 2020. "Opinion: Urbanism is Complicit in Infra-Structural Racism — And Reparations Have a Place in the Built Environment." *USA Streetsblog.* 27 July. Accessed 19 July 2024. Available at: https://usa.streetsblog.org/2020/07/27/opinion-urbanism-is-complicit-in-infra-structural-racism-and-reparations-have-a-place-in-the-built-environment.

About np:

Dedicated to the formation of the social and economic combinations of new presses, the nonprofit np: (np-press.org) creates new institutionally-based publishing units. It questions how innovation comes about in scholarly publishing, given the speed of technological change and the quickly modified forms by which knowledge is arrived at and sustained. Many publishers continue to over-rely on outmoded communication technologies and assumptions about what content is and how it is generated. np: is designed specifically to circumvent the problematic nature of publication as we know it, including not simply the way current practices shape scholarship but also the tendency toward reproducing inequality and exclusion.

As part of its program, np: publishes, hosts, and supports work that interrogates the university system and its sedimented histories, from land acquisition to student debt. np:'s standpoint is decisively outside the university press framework and so activates new perspectives on academic labor, knowledge production, and modes of resistance.